Ecosystems and Health: a UK Perspective

**EDITED BY CONOR LINSTEAD,
ROGER CROFTS AND EDWARD MALTBY**

Mary Sibthorp

Mary Sibthorp (1905–1991) was a remarkable person. Largely self-educated, her incisive intellect allowed her to hold more than her own in any discussion. In her twenties, she came to the notice of Lord Davies of Llandinam, a fighter for peace and a better world order. She worked with him until his death in 1944 and thereafter continued to work for his New Commonwealth Society. When the David Davies Memorial Institute of International Studies was founded in 1951 she became its Assistant Secretary and in due course the Director, a post she held until her retirement in 1980. Together with her outstanding characteristics of iconoclasm, dislike of utopianism and her suspicion of received wisdom, her energy and inspiring vision had great influence on the work of the Institute. She was much interested in the wise use of, and the international problems arising from, the use of natural resources. In her generous will Mary left instructions to set up the Sibthorp Trust, which sponsored this seminar.

The Sibthorp Trust

A specific aim of the Sibthorp Trust is to promote the discussion of key environmental issues through the commissioning of workshops, seminars and study groups and to publish the results of these activities.

The Trustees hosted the First Sibthorp Seminar in 1996 entitled 'Advances in ecological science as a basis for conservation and ecosystem management in the third millennium'. The outcomes from this seminar were captured in the book Ecosystem Management: Questions for Science and Society. This was published in 1999 and played a key role in the early development of the Ecosystem Approach, which was subsequently adopted by the Conference of Parties to the Convention on Biological Diversity as the fundamental tool for delivery of the Convention's primary objectives.

The Second Sibthorp Seminar considered the question 'Do conservation targets help?' This seminar topic was based on an article published in Science by Soulé and Sanjayan, but broadened to take a wider look at nature conservation in the light of the major changes that have taken place since the mid 20th Century and which have influenced our underlying assumptions about conservation: the internationalisation of the conservation agenda following Agenda 21 and the coming into force of the Convention on Biological Diversity, the widespread adoption of the aim of sustainable development, the different time scales of concern, demographic growth, climate change, and the changing relationships between science, society and government. The outputs from the seminar were published in 2006 as Do conservation targets help?

From these different influences come various agendas, and the aims, goals and priorities proposed by the conservation and biodiversity communities may not be recognised or accepted by other constituencies. The seminar examined and discussed these various perspectives and, where necessary, challenged them and attempted to see how far these often conflicting aims may be reconciled.

In this Third Sibthorp Seminar we take a critical look at the evidence for the link between ecosystems and human health and examine some of the policy implications of these links for the UK. It is hoped that the more forward-looking the discussion in the following chapters is, and the more it focuses on unsound viewpoints, the better it will fulfill Mary's purpose.

Acknowledgements

The editors would like to thank Linda Jones for her work in transcribing the recordings of the seminar, the authors of the chapters for devoting their time to presenting and writing their papers and the participants of the seminar for their valuable contributions to the discussion.

Published by the Sibthorp Trust, Liverpool, UK
Copyright © The Sibthorp Trust 2009

Citation: Linstead, C., Crofts, R. and Maltby, E. (2009)
Ecosystems and Health: a UK perspective. The Sibthorp Trust, Liverpool, UK

DESIGN: MIKE CARNEY. WWW.MIKESSTUDIO.CO.UK
PHOTOGRAPHY © MIKE CARNEY AND GETTY IMAGES.

ISBN 978-0-9554096-1-5

Contents

Foreword

CONOR LINSTEAD, UNIVERSITY OF LIVERPOOL

Ecosystems and Human Health: a UK perspective captures the outputs from the Third Sibthorp Seminar held by the Sibthorp Trust in July 2007. The aim of the seminar was to take a critical look at the evidence for the link between ecosystems and human health and examine some of the policy implications of these links for the UK. This is a fast changing and increasingly important area, and has significant implications for the policies and practices of many sectors from health to conservation and agriculture. The links between ecosystems and health cover a wide spectrum of issues and so, to focus the discussion, the seminar concentrated on three key aspects of this broad topic: the influence of access to green spaces and nature on well-being; the current and potential future threats to human health from diseases in the wild that can be transmitted to humans; and the role of ecosystems in reducing the exposure of people to pollutants and pathogens. Within this framework, the topics covered during the seminar were wide-ranging and, taken as a whole, attempt to give a broad overview of the technical and scientific disciplines that are relevant to the linkage between ecosystems and human health in a UK context. Key presentations from the seminar have been included in this book as written papers. The conclusions chapter draws together the common threads of the papers and subsequent seminar discussion to present some overarching observations that span the ecosystem and health topic.

The contributions to this book show that there are clear mental and physical health benefits from contact with natural ecosystems and green spaces (see Stone, Chapter 2; Bird, Chapter 3; and Peacock, Chapter 4). But there are also negative health impacts from increased contact with nature, in particular from zoonoses, pollutants and pathogens, although properly functioning ecosystems do regulate the exposure of people to these hazards (Bell, Chapter 6; Linstead and Maltby, Chapter 9). The risks of zoonoses with wild hosts are low in the UK compared with other countries, certainly in terms of the number of zoonoses that are of concern but also in terms of seriousness (Hart, Chapter 5). Although the recent pandemic of the swine influenza virus is potentially one of the highest risk zoonoses that have been faced recently in the UK, it does not have strong link with natural ecosystems. It is interesting to note that the potential risks of influenza viruses from animal hosts other than birds (avian influenza was of particular concern at the time of the Sibthorp workshop and this does have a strong link with natural ecosystems) was highlighted by Hart in Chapter 5, well in advance of the recent swine influenza virus pandemic.

A key theme emerging from the seminar is the importance of maintaining the integrity of ecosystems to achieve health benefits and reduce the risks from pathogens, zoonoses or pollutants. Changes to ecosystem structure, either from direct intervention or indirectly through climate change, are likely to increase the occurrence and spread of some zoonoses. Reducing the complexity of the ecosystems that people interact with is also likely to reduce the potential for mental health benefits and the way we manage ecosystems influences the pathways and exposure routes for pathogens and pollutants. Pickup (Chapter 7) discusses an example of how the pathways of a pathogen (*Mycobacterium avium* subspecies *paratuberculosis,* MAP) through the environment are influenced by the interaction of agriculture with the water supply system. Sinnett and Hutchings (Chapter 8) give examples of how vegetation can have a strong influence on the pathways of pollutants.

Maintaining healthy ecosystems can also help to create a more resilient society. For example, Linstead and Maltby (Chapter 9) discuss how wetland ecosystems can increase the resilience of the water supply system by improving and buffering water quality, both in terms of chemical quality and pathogens. Although no research has been done, perhaps wetlands have a key role to play in influencing the pathways of MAP, and other pathogens, through the environment.

This tension between the negative and positive aspects of people interacting with natural ecosystems may be one of the key barriers to greater encouragement of access to nature as a therapeutic treatment. On one hand there are the dangers of accidents, pollutants and zoonoses, which are low risk (in the UK at least) but can be high impact, and on the other hand there are the benefits, which are much more difficult to quantify and predict for an individual and are diffuse and intangible, such that they can only be easily observed at a group or community level. The benefits of encouraging greater interaction with nature can, however, potentially be very large when aggregated across the entire population. This lack of ability to define a precise dose-response relationship does not sit well with the emphasis within the medical profession on intervention with drugs or surgery rather than prevention and 'softer' treatments. When faced with the perception of risk and the difficultly in precisely quantifying or predicting the benefits it is all too easy to resort to traditional approaches for cases where, perhaps, prescribing health walks instead of or alongside such approaches may have a better and more sustainable outcome.

It is of vital importance, therefore, that the case why ecosystem management matters for human health is made strongly, and where possible in economic terms, to all the relevant sectors of society and government. In particular, the multifarious services provided by ecosystems need to be recognised across all government departments and its agencies so that ecosystem management is not just seen as a priority in those departments with a conservation or environmental remit, and resources are allocated accordingly.

1

Links between Nature and Health

DAVID STONE, NATURAL ENGLAND

1.1 Introduction

There is a growing recognition that access to and contact with nature is important for peoples' long-term health and well-being. A link between nature and health feels intuitively right but is there more to it than that? Is there an added 'health value' that cannot be replicated in the gym? Do we get something extra from engaging with nature as part of our everyday lives, whether that is in our local urban green space or on top of the Cumbrian Fells? This chapter examines the case for it being more than just a nice idea to get outdoors through an exploration of the evidence-base linking nature and health. Specifically it addresses four key questions:

- Where does the concept of a link between nature and health come from?
- Does the natural environment have any human health utility?
- Does the natural environment determine human health?
- Is it important to have a biologically diverse natural environment for good human health?

These questions are explored in the context of the UK, a developed first-world country. The demands of modern urban life can make it seem that the natural environment is something remote and without influence on our lives. People are generally not engaged with nature. Nature is the birds, insects and plants of television documentaries, not part our everyday life. This disengagement leads to a perception that people are not part of the natural world and that it has no influence upon us, but we are far closer to the natural world than is credited and this link affects our health.

Human evolution provides a useful starting point for considering the notion of nature and health. Our evolutionary ancestors *Australopithecus* lived approximately 3 to 4 million years ago. Initially forest dwelling, *Australopithecus* evolved into a plains dweller, and then about 2 million years ago into *Homo habilis*, a species that lived in a variety of habitats. *Homo sapiens sapiens* appeared approximately 200,000 years ago, but it is only in the last 10,000 years that man has pursued agriculture and developed urban civilisations (Baldia, 2003). For the vast majority of our evolutionary history our ancestors were very much engaged with and shaped by their natural environment. *Homo sapiens sapiens* has slowly evolved in response to the natural environments and habitats it encountered. It can be argued that the changes to our environment over the last 10,000 years due to agriculture, urbanisation and industrialisation has been too rapid for us to have completely adapted to them by biological evolutionary processes. Biological scientists, ecologists and natural historians recognise the importance of an organism's environment to its health, and if that environment changes they are quick to recognise and document the resulting physiological stress, reduced fecundity, increased mortality, increased disease burden and, in extreme cases, extinction. Given our evolution, are people really different? Can we continue to thrive if the environment to which we are adapted fundamentally and rapidly changes? Does urbanicity threaten our health?

The idea that we are intimately linked with nature was articulated clearly by E O Wilson when he argued in *Biophilia* (1984) that we have an innate sensitivity to, and need for, living things because we have existed in a close relationship with nature for most of our evolution. We should not consider ourselves as fundamentally different to other species and our links with nature are core to our well-being. E O Wilson was not the first to put forward such ideas. They have long been around in different forms. Hippocrates' essay *On Airs, Waters and Places* from 300 BC is one of the earliest writings to consider the influence of climate, water and situation on health and how people's well-being is intimately linked with the environment. From these early written beginnings the idea has continued to the present day.

The public health movement was founded on the recognition of these same links. John Snow's (1813–1854) work on cholera was based on an understanding that polluted or contaminated environments were a source of ill health and water can be a transport mechanism for infectious diseases. He published *The Mode of Communication of Cholera* in 1849, which suggested the waterborne nature of the disease, but many still refused to abandon the 'miasma' (bad air) theory which held that cholera was a product of the poor air quality in urban areas, although this theory was also founded, albeit incorrectly, on ideas of environment and health connections. He proved his theory through the investigation of and prohibition of the Broad Street pump in Soho towards the end of August 1854.

Those visionaries of the Victorian health movement were often looking at degraded and polluted environments. Nevertheless, they were very conscious of the relationship between the environment and health outcomes. Bringing the story up to date, and still from a public health perspective, Barton and Grant (2006) have revised the classic public health model of Dahlgren and Whitehead (1991) (Figure 1-1). This new model focuses more on the determinants on health at an individual level and incorporates issues related to global ecosystems, climatic change and biodiversity. Within this model the role of the natural environment as a determining factor is explicitly acknowledged and given greater emphasis, but it is retained in the context of the other key drivers of health such as lifestyle, community and economy. These links are identified in the Millennium Ecosystem Assessment (MEA, 2005) as being particularly important for developing countries but they are equally applicable to society in the UK. An important aspect of the model from Barton and Grant (2006) is that it does not imply directionality: environmental determinants can have a positive or a negative influence on an individual's health outcomes.

FIGURE 1-1
Public health model of Barton and Grant (2006)

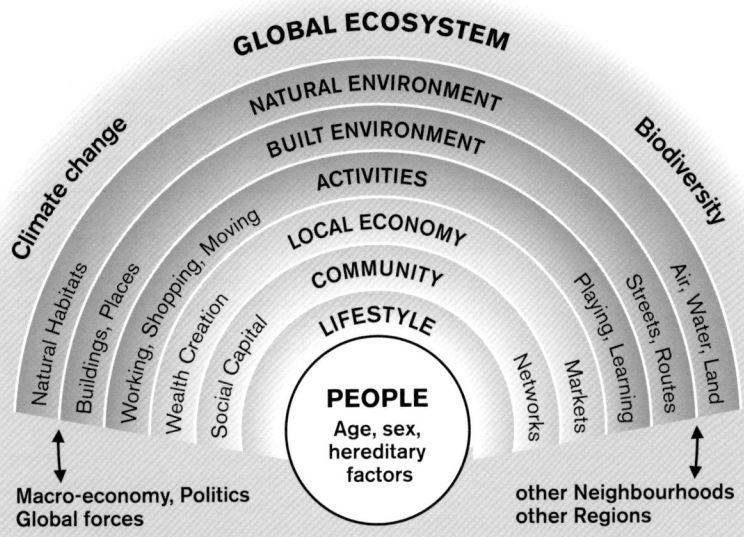

The determinants of health and well-being in our neighbourhoods

1.2 Mechanisms linking nature and health

There is, then, a credible theoretical basis that links human health and nature, drawn from the biological and public health sciences. This serves as a foundation for dialogue between these different communities that can help to develop these ideas further into practical actions that can improve people's well-being. The need for practical actions is becoming more and more apparent. We are increasingly sedentary and increasingly urban. In 2008 the human species officially became an urban species, with more people living in cities than in rural areas. Humans have, wittingly or unwittingly, changed their behaviour and their habitat. We have disconnected ourselves from nature, which is giving rise to some serious emerging health issues.

What that means for the UK, which has already gone through many of the changes now being seen elsewhere in the world associated with a rural to urban transition and increased wealth, is increasing mental ill-health and physical ill-health due to inactivity. These changes in lifestyle and habitat have significant financial and social costs. The estimated cost of depression in England is £7.5 billion per year (McCrone *et al.* 2007). The cost of physical ill-health due to inactivity, such as diabetes and obesity, is estimated by the Department of Health to be £8.2 billion per year (DoH 2004a). Although certainly not all of these costs are due to our disconnection from the natural environment, a significant proportion of it is (see Chapters 2 and 3) and these costs could be reduced by increased contact with nature.

Extreme weather events attributed to climate change, or which act as analogues for future climate change, are emphasising the link between our health and nature in the most extreme ways. In the 2003 heat wave there were an additional 32,000 deaths in Europe and an increase in hospital admissions by 16% over the long term average, with 46% of those increase admissions being directly attributable to the heat (Kovats and Jendritzky, 2006). The convergence of changes in lifestyle and changes in climate are posing new and increased health pressures, for which those who understand the links between nature and health can offer some options for mitigation and adaptation. Public health professionals have recognised that access to good quality natural environments may well be part of the solution to addressing the rising costs of healthcare. Environmentalists have recognised that they have more to offer society than just saving distant rain forests.

There are two perspectives on nature and its relationship to health. We can look at nature in terms of its utility for physical and mental health of individuals and as an agent for the determination of health of the wider population. The health utility of nature, in the sense used here, is the ability to access the natural environment through individual action. Pretty *et al.* (2005a) identified three ways in which people obtain this utility: passive (e.g. viewing), incidental (e.g. cycling through) and active (e.g. conservation work). The determination of health from nature comes from involuntary exposure to the influences of or services of the natural environment that effect health outcomes of individuals, communities, and populations. This is exemplified by the provision of water free from pollutants and pathogens through processes of natural filtration.

1.3 Natural environment and human health utility

There has been a range of work looking at the health utility of the natural environment (e.g. Sempik *et al.* 2002; Maller *et al.* 2002; Pretty *et al.* 2005a; Boldeman *et al.* 2004). The effects identified by this research can be categorised into effects on physical health and effects on mental health. The physical effects found include stress reduction and increased levels of physical activity (particularly in children) leading to a reduction in factors contributing to cardio-vascular disease, rheumatoid arthritis, diabetes, ulcers and hypertension. Mental health effects, which can be as important as physical effects, include improvement in self-esteem, alleviation of anxiety, self-awareness, addiction rehabilitation, reduced psychosis and developed social capital. These benefits can contribute to the delivery of three identified health priorities in the UK: reduction of cancers, improved mental well-being and reduction of heart disease. The evidence provides a tangible case that enables policy makers to modify policies and guidance, enhance their effectiveness, and increase health outcome delivery through the natural environment. Incorporating these cost effective and preventative measures into health programmes is becoming increasingly important as healthcare costs continue to rise with an ageing and generally less healthy population (Wanless 2002).

The underlying mechanisms for the health effects of natural environments have been explained through psycho-physiological stress recovery theory (Ulrich *et al.* 1991) and attention restoration theory (Kaplan 1995; Kaplan and Kaplan 1995). These mechanisms are explored further by Bird in Chapter 3. Importantly, these ideas do not come from the natural sciences but from psychologists and others within the medical profession.

Mind (2007) looked at the percentage of people who experienced improvement, no change or worsening of feelings of self-esteem, depression and tension following outdoor and indoor walks. The results showed a significantly higher proportion of people found an improvement in all three areas following outdoor walks compared with indoor walks and significantly larger proportion of people found a worsening following indoor walks compared with outdoor walks. This effect is in line with the results of other studies that have examined aspects of mental health and the outdoors, such as Hartig *et al.* (2003) or Herzog (1997) and reinforces the importance of having contact with nature as part of exercise treatments for mental health conditions.

1.4 Natural environment health determination

Looking at the urban environment, where we often feel the natural environment has little influence on us, Takano *et al.* (2002) demonstrated clearly that accessible green space increases longevity in Tokyo. This was one of the few studies that have looked at this relationship with a large enough sample size and over a large enough area to exclude confounding variables from the data. Giles-Corti *et al.* (2005) looked at the relationships between accessible natural environments and physical activity and found that high densities of accessible natural environments, including urban parks, increased levels of physical activity. In children, Boldeman *et al.* (2004) found that more complex open spaces, in terms of the landscape structure and levels of biodiversity, increased overall activity and reduced ultra violet radiation exposure. Taking a broader community level assessment, de Vries *et al.* (2003) found in the Netherlands that having nature and green spaces nearby correlated with better physical and mental health outcomes, fewer GP visits and increased self-evaluation of health in the local area. Mitchell and Popham (2008) found that exposure to natural environments affected health inequalities in the working-age population of England. They concluded that health inequalities related to income deprivation were reduced in the poorest populations exposed to the greenest environments. In the urban context, therefore, there is a good deal of evidence that the quality of the environment helps to improve health and this effect is detectable at both a community and an individual level.

In a UK context, Midgely *et al.* (2005) found a strong correlation between health, environment and deprivation in the North West of England. In this study a range of environmental indicators were used to quantify the environment ranging from the area of National Nature Reserves to air quality measures. This study stresses the importance of functional ecosystems, even in urban areas, to improve environmental quality. This is important not just from visual and activity perspective, as stressed in studies from health professionals, but also but also in terms of the other ecosystem services that improve the quality of people's environment, often in ways unnoticed by individuals. These services include catchment and flood plain management (see Chapter 8), micro-climate moderation and particulate trapping. While damage from flooding is often viewed as an extreme but acute event, those affected have months of physical and mental stress to deal with after the event. Undoubtedly, given what we have learned, there will be peaks in disease with communities affected by flooding in the months that follow it.

The World Health Organisation (2005) has recognised the importance for human health of biodiversity as a source of medicines, for the environmental services it provides and its value for bio indicators. Pongsiri and Roman (2007) noted that 'changes in biodiversity can profoundly impact the ability of ecosystems to provide clean water, energy, food, recreation, and other services that contribute to human well-being' and recognised that changes to ecosystems can affect the transmission of infectious diseases to people, in particular vector borne diseases such as malaria and Lyme disease. Until recently cases of malaria identified in Europe were contracted abroad, but there have recently been cases of malaria in Southern Europe that originated within Europe itself (Baldari 1998). It is thought that these cases originated because of a change in the species of mosquito, with alien carrier species replacing endemic species. Shifting climatic zones due to warming are removing the ecological barriers to the distribution of the ticks largely responsible for the transmission of Lyme disease, leading to an increased incidence of the disease in Northern Europe (Lindgren and Jaenson 2006).

Public health professionals are becoming more aware of the link between natural ecosystems and health outcomes and are increasingly arguing for ecosystem protection and sustainable lifestyles on the basis of its health implications. In this way, there is a convergence of argument from the perspective of natural scientists and public health professionals, although the differences in terminology between the two disciplines still presents a barrier to greater progress. However, environmentalists are interested in preserving attributes of the environment such as wildness, rarity, uniqueness and biodiversity so can this convergence actually reach common ground? Does a reasonable facsimile of a natural ecosystem have the physical and mental health benefits without the need for preserving those attributes environmentalists hold dear?

Establishing whether the degree of biological diversity is important in the link between nature and health is a key part of determining whether there can be common ground between health professionals and environmentalists. Fuller et al. (2007) looked at the connection between psychological well-being, in terms of attributes such as reflection and distinct identity, and biodiversity value as measured by species richness and habitat heterogeneity. The study found a significant relationship ($p < 0.005$) in these mental health attributes as the biodiversity indicators increase.

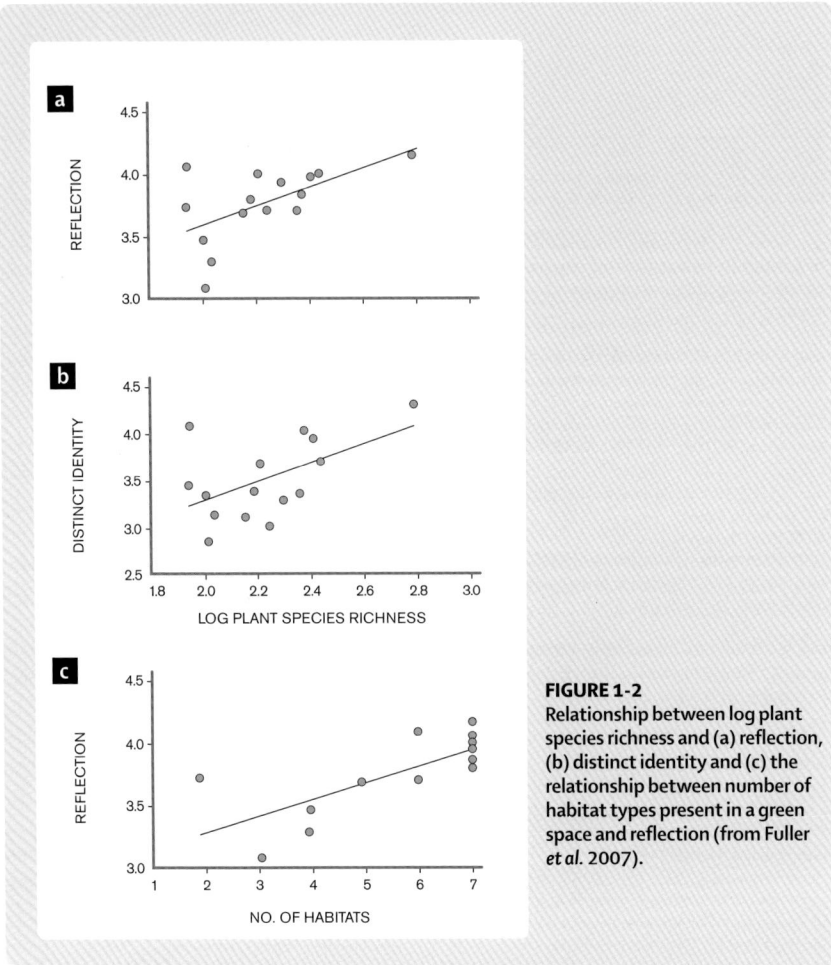

FIGURE 1-2
Relationship between log plant species richness and (a) reflection, (b) distinct identity and (c) the relationship between number of habitat types present in a green space and reflection (from Fuller *et al.* 2007).

Other experimental work testing psychological restoration against degree of naturalness has also found a significant negative correlation between biodiversity and stress (Staats and Hartig 2004; van den Berg *et al.* 2007; Ulrich *et al.* 1991). It does appear, therefore, that the degree of biodiversity is important in this relationship and health professionals and those concerned with preserving natural environments can work towards a common goal. However, the degree to which increasing access to natural environments compromises biodiversity and there is therefore a trade-off between these two ecosystem services remains an area that needs further investigation.

1.5 Conclusions

We can form robust arguments from both an environmental perspective and from a public health perspective that the natural environment has a utility value for human physical and mental health. This effect can be seen at an individual level and at a community level and a richness of biodiversity appears to be an important part of maintaining the functional integrity required to support positive health outcomes.

However, there are some research gaps. The vast majority of research in the area of environment and health has focused on the negative consequences of degraded and contaminated environments. Therefore, many of the arguments behind protecting or enhancing nature for health benefits are either based on the negative consequences of further environmental degradation or are extrapolations of improvements we would expect through enhancement drawn from negative health impact results.

Although there is evidence that a relationship exists between the level of biodiversity and the effect on health, we know very little of the mechanisms that underpin it. To engage with health professionals, natural scientists need to learn to construct their arguments within the paradigms used by health professionals and further investigations in this relationship need to be presented within the 'dose-response' context they work within.

We need better information on the cost effectiveness of our interventions. The costs of conventional health treatments are relatively easy to define compared with the costs of maintaining an area of green space and establishing the precise health benefits of that space. Looking at the evidence that has been presented here, it seems likely that maintaining green spaces would be a cost effective form of health treatment but the cost-effectiveness evidence is not fully developed.

At a larger scale, we need to be very clear about the potential effects of climate change on human health. It seems plausible that maintaining healthy ecosystems can mitigate the effects of climate change by regulating local climates.

The idea that natural ecosystems have positive benefits for health is a relatively new one for policy-makers. In order to ensure that these new ideas feed into policy, researchers and practitioners need to avoid the 'nature and health' research area becoming an isolated discipline. Natural scientists need to engage with health researchers and professionals and both groups need to engage fully with policy makers. We need to be broad in our thinking and recognise other social determinants of health and their interactions with the effects of nature. We must avoid making claims that the health effect of ecosystems can solve all of our health problems. In reality, it is just one part of the solution, but a part that must not be overlooked.

2

Green Exercise:
Policy Implications for
Health and Nature

JO PEACOCK, UNIVERSITY OF ESSEX

2.1 Introduction

Conserving the natural environment and improving the health of the nation are pivotal government and public priorities. Current concerns about the combined adverse health effects of modern diets and sedentary lifestyles are continually emerging. Participating in regular physical activity is accepted as a highly effective method for preventing illness and is an important determinant of both physical health and psychological well-being. However, daily levels of physical activity are rapidly declining, despite the robust evidence for the importance of staying active. This is a contributory factor in the increasing number of cases of preventable health problems such as obesity, diabetes, heart disease and certain cancers. Today, we expend 500 kcal less energy per day in comparison to our ancestors fifty years ago. This equates to doing a marathon a week less exercise, mainly because our lifestyles have become so sedentary, both at work and during our leisure time.

We have suffered very significant public health consequences as a result of this activity transition. The annual costs of physical inactivity in England are reported by the Department of Health to be approximately £8.2 billion (DoH 2004a). This figure excludes individuals who are obese due to inactivity, which contributes an extra £2.5 billion annual cost to the economy. The Department of Health have estimated that a ten percent increase in adult physical activity alone would benefit the UK by £500 million per year and save six thousand lives.

The prevalence of mental illness in the UK is also increasing rapidly and there is growing evidence that stress and mental ill-health have become substantial health problems for many cohorts of people. It is believed that at least one in six individuals suffer from a 'significant' mental health problem at any one time and some reports quote this figure as high as one in four. Sufferers of anxiety and depression are commonplace and by 2020 it is predicted that depression will be the second most common cause of disability in the developed world. Mental illness is not solely a challenge for the health sector to address as it inflicts wider economic and social costs. It is estimated that the total costs of mental illness in England in 2002–03 were approximately £77.4 billion (The Sainsbury Centre for Mental Health 2003).

Evidence now shows that there is also a positive relationship between exposure to nature and mental and physical health (Pretty 2007). The key message emerging is that contact with nature improves psychological health by reducing stress levels, enhancing mood and offering a restorative environment that enables people to relax, unwind and recharge their batteries. Establishing an emotional connection with the environment also inspires us to think about, and become engaged with environmental issues such as conservation and climate change and promotes environmentally friendly behaviours. Green space rich in biodiversity not only provides the ideal opportunity for outdoor recreation and acts as a valuable health resource for its users, but also initiates a virtuous cycle of benefit to the environment itself. As nature makes such positive contributions to our health we should encourage others to get active outdoors, so that they can connect to each other as well as to nature.

2.2 The concept of green exercise

There is a growing body of empirical evidence which shows that exposure to nature induces substantial mental health benefits. Equally, participating in physical activity is known to result in positive physical and mental health outcomes. Therefore, at the University of Essex we have combined these ideas into a programme of research investigating the synergistic benefits of participating in physical activities whilst being exposed to nature. We refer to this as "green exercise" (Figure 2-1). This programme addresses current concerns about the adverse health effects of modern diets and sedentary lifestyles, along with growing evidence that stress and mental ill-health have become substantial health problems for many people in industrialised societies.

Our health is also shaped by our diets and our connections to other people. We have seen a nutrition transition in our diets, which has had serious consequences for our health. There has been a large increase in diet-related chronic diseases in adults, but now more worryingly also in children, and the prevalence of obesity has become a major problem. Our connections to other people helps to increase social capital, which is defined by a sense of neighbourliness, relationships with trust, reciprocity, and having many social groups and established networks that bind people together. Healthy communities have higher levels of social capital and where there is greater interaction between people in the community there is a greater sense of 'community spirit'.

So, together these four components lead to improvements in our physical health and emotional well-being which leads to healthier communities and avoided public health costs. However, to maximise this potential we need to strive to change people's behaviour forever. We want to encourage people to participate in green exercise activities continually rather than indulging in the experience for a short while and then reverting back to their previous behaviour. We want the changes to their lifestyles and behaviours sustained in the long term, in order to capitalise on the health dividends.

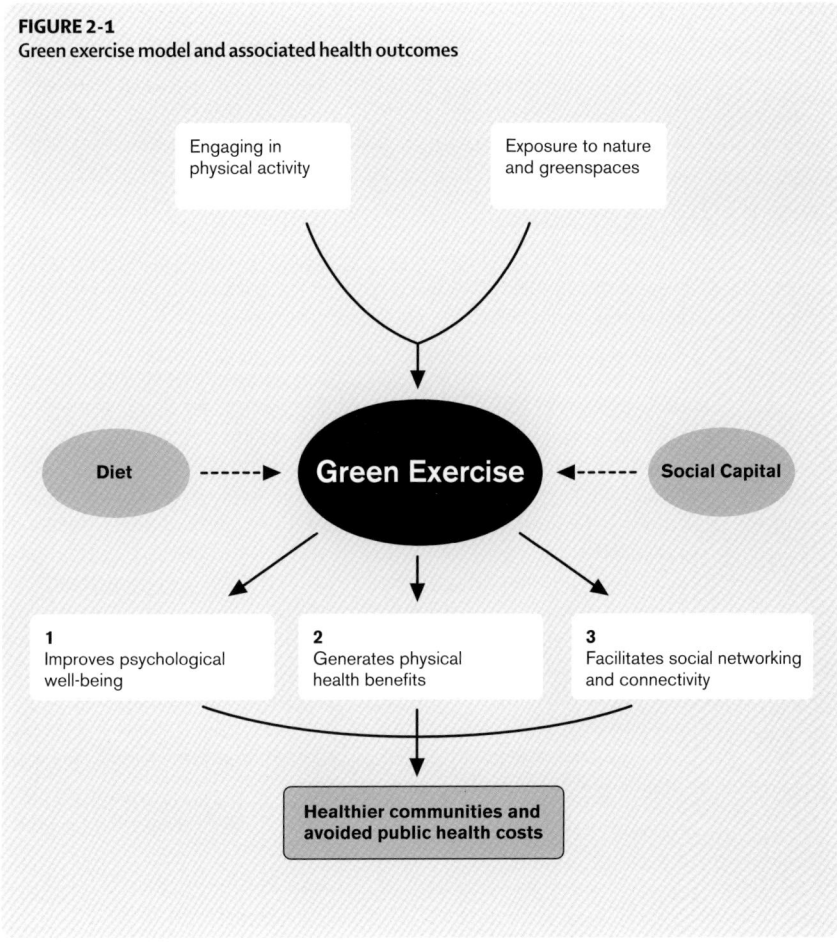

FIGURE 2-1
Green exercise model and associated health outcomes

Engaging in physical activity

Exposure to nature and greenspaces

Diet

Green Exercise

Social Capital

1 Improves psychological well-being

2 Generates physical health benefits

3 Facilitates social networking and connectivity

Healthier communities and avoided public health costs

2.3 The evidence base

From a wide variety of research, we have discerned three broad health outcomes from participating in green exercise: 1) improvement of psychological well-being (by enhancing mood and self-esteem, whilst reducing feelings of anger, confusion, depression and tension); 2) generation of physical health benefits (by reducing blood pressure and burning calories) and 3) facilitation of social networking and connectivity (by enhancing social capital).

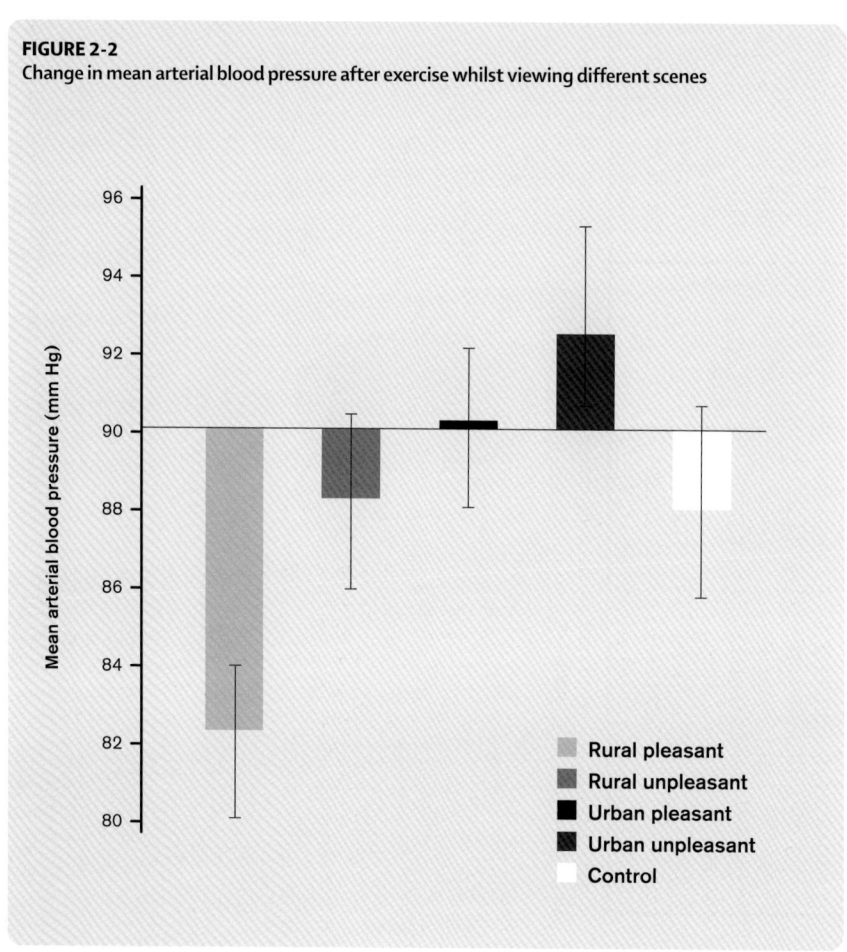

FIGURE 2-2
Change in mean arterial blood pressure after exercise whilst viewing different scenes

Proof of principle was initially established in a laboratory, where 100 subjects exercised on a treadmill whilst viewing a series of rural or urban pleasant and unpleasant pictures. An 8.7% decrease in blood pressure was reported after exercising whilst viewing rural pleasant pictures compared with a 1.9% decrease when faced with a blank screen and a 3.3% increase in blood pressure after viewing urban unpleasant pictures (Figure 2-2). All pleasant green scenes enhanced mood and self-esteem in comparison to unpleasant pictures lacking nature (Pretty et al. 2005b). Our findings suggest that exercising in pleasant green environments has a greater effect than exercise alone on blood pressure, mental health and well-being.

The benefits of green exercise were analysed in the field by studying 263 subjects engaging in different types of outdoor activities (walking, cycling, fishing, nature conservation, woodland activities, horse-riding and boating) at 10 locations in the UK (Pretty *et al.* 2005b, 2006 and 2007). Participants were found to be significantly less angry, depressed, confused and tense after engaging in the activities and the self-esteem levels of all significantly improved. This was an impressive finding considering the sample population were already choosing to engage in activities so were reasonably healthy to start with. These improvements were not affected by the type, intensity, or duration of the green exercise activity, indicating the potential for a wider health and well-being dividend from many types of green exercise.

The health benefits of environmental improvements at three green sites in the UK, involving urban park and canal regeneration schemes, were measured in 92 local users. The environmental improvements encouraged more people to visit the sites, to visit more frequently and to spend longer engaging with nature on each visit. Significantly more people visited the improved sites for exercise, health, scenery and wildlife, as opposed to just using it as a thoroughfare to get to work or school, or because it happened to be the nearest space to walk the dog. The number of visits increased but, more importantly, the improved environments started to attract *new* visitors.

We have also investigated the multifunctionality of five iconic sites in Essex and Suffolk. Engaging in green exercise activities at the sites increased self-esteem and significantly reduced feelings of anger, depression and tension in a survey of 159 visitors. The majority of sites were perceived to be important for wildlife biodiversity, landscape character, scenery, leisure and recreation. However, less than half of the visitors felt the sites were important for health, so even though they were spending hours walking within beautiful green settings, they did not appear to acknowledge its influence on their well-being. These areas should however be recognised for their role in enhancing physical health and psychological well-being in addition to the fundamental part they play in helping to conserve our natural environment and heritage.

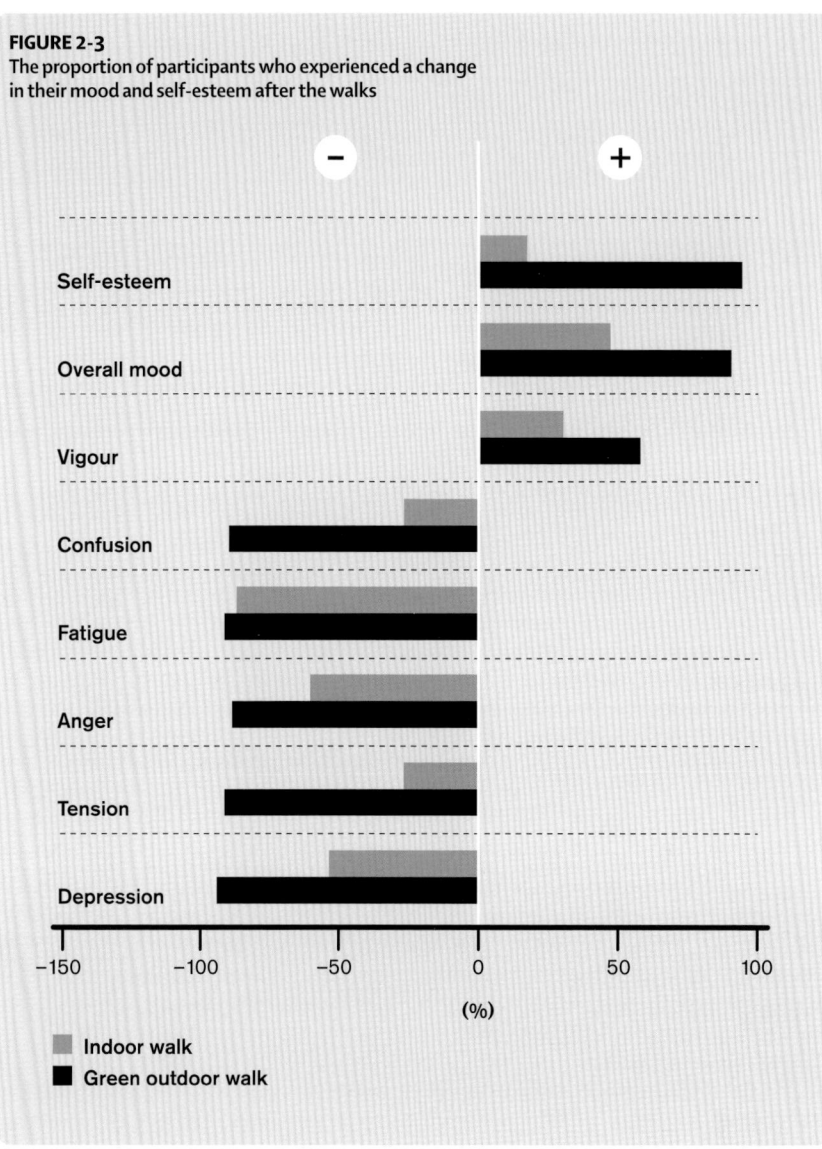

FIGURE 2-3
The proportion of participants who experienced a change
in their mood and self-esteem after the walks

We have assessed the role the environment plays in the effectiveness of exercise for mental well-being with members of local Mind groups. Members participated in both a green outdoor walk and an indoor shopping-mall walk, both of which were for the same amount of time. Improvements in self-esteem and mood were significantly greater following the green outdoor walk in comparison to the equivalent indoor walk, especially for feelings of anger, depression and tension (Mind 2007 and Figure 2-3). For this group of mental health service users, exercising outdoors in a green environment was better than comparable exercise indoors. It was more enjoyable, more therapeutic and had a positive effect on participants' mental health and well-being.

This kind of evidence suggests that therapeutic applications of green exercise activities may be effective, and we refer to this as 'green care'. Thus, we have designed a feasibility study to compare green exercise and cognitive behavioural therapy as treatment options for patients suffering from mild-moderate depression. We are also conducting a small pilot study to analyse the psychological health benefits of participating in a series of weekly green walks for people experiencing a range of mental health problems. We are working with a wilderness foundation to assess the mental health benefits and connectedness of individuals to nature during wilderness excursions. We are also investigating the impact of environmental volunteering on the connectedness of individuals to nature, and their behaviours and attitudes to the environment.

The University of Essex is a partner in the National Care Farming Initiative and is undertaking research to ascertain the range and number of care farming initiatives currently operating in the UK, and their effects on psychological health and well-being. Green care in agriculture or care farming is defined as the use of farms and agricultural landscapes as a base for promoting mental and physical health. Farming activities are used to provide mental and physical health benefits for a wide range of people including those with defined medical or social needs (e.g. psychiatric patients, those suffering from mild to moderate depression, people with learning disabilities, people with a history of drug abuse, disaffected youth or elderly people) as well as those suffering from the effects of work-related stress or ill-health arising from obesity. Care farming is a partnership between farmers, health care providers and participants, and so combines the care of people with the care of the land.

We have shown that green exercise brings substantial mental and physical health benefits for a variety of different subject cohorts in the UK. Our findings suggest that priority should be given to developing the use of green exercise as a therapeutic intervention (green care). Such evidence, though, has yet to influence substantially urban and rural planning, priorities for public health, social care and criminal justice programmes, or recommendations for development of sustainable lifestyles.

2.4 Policy implications

Green exercise and green care have a multitude of important policy implications for a wide range of rural and urban sectors. It is clear that a large number of people already use the countryside and urban green spaces for leisure activities, from which they derive a health benefit. However, physical and mental health problems are on the increase and many people do not access green spaces at all. We therefore face two key challenges: 1) to increase the number of people participating in green exercise, especially those suffering from ill-health due to their sedentary lifestyles, and those not accessing the countryside or green spaces for recreation and leisure; 2) to increase the rate of use by those already participating in green exercise. This can be addressed through improved provision and access and by wider recognition that exposure both to nature and green space and to physical activity in those environments should be a central part of the policies and strategies of a large number of organisations.

To spread the message we also need to encourage working in partnership. For example, countryside and land agencies should advertise the health benefits of their resources, and health agencies should advertise the mental and physical health benefits of activities in rural and urban green spaces. Establishing the link between the environmental and health sectors is vitally important to foster collaborative working partnerships at all governmental levels.

Increasing support for and access to a wide range of green exercise activities for all sectors of society should produce substantial economic and public health benefits as well as reducing individual human suffering. Therefore, it seems evident that promoting participation in both green exercise activities and green care has important implications for public and environmental health.

The health sector

The health sector needs to consider the contribution that green exercise makes to both individual health and public well-being. Health professionals at Primary Care Trust level, including GPs, should work closely with other sectors to publicise the link between health and the environment more effectively. Environmental, countryside, sports and planning professionals can all be involved in affecting the mental and physical health of local communities in partnership with the health sector. Ultimately, a fitter, happier population has the potential to make substantial savings for the National Health Service.

Future Physical Activity Plans should emphasise the value of nature and green space for formal and informal use, and also stress the therapeutic value of the outdoors (both rural and urban) for delivering mental well-being and encouraging physical activity. GPs should be encouraged to consider and recognise the value of 'green prescriptions', especially for those leading sedentary lifestyles. Green exercise should also be recognised as a clinically valid treatment option for patients experiencing mental distress. A recommendation to take part in existing local green exercise activities is a relatively cheap and effective way for primary health care practitioners to encourage people to become more active and reconnect to nature.

Health professionals can play a key role in disseminating the information as part of a health care package, as they have regular contact with patients. However, at present there is a lack of knowledge and acceptance of the benefits among GPs, and providers of health and social care need to be encouraged to take the idea of green care more seriously. Research conducted by the Mental Health Foundation has found that only 5% of GPs offer exercise therapy as one of their three most common treatment responses for mild to moderate depression. By comparison, 93% commonly prescribe antidepressants. Many have admitted to prescribing antidepressants in situations where they did not believe this was the most effective approach, but because they did not have access to other options (Halliwell 2005). This highlights the need for an easily accessible directory of existing project details to enhance their knowledge and understanding of local opportunities.

Another major problem in encouraging more 'green prescriptions' is to overcome the patient's perceptions, where they exist, of green exercise not being an effective treatment response. Sometimes, patients subconsciously believe that taking a pill will automatically make them feel better, whereas leaving their doctor's surgery with a recommendation to engage in regular outdoor walks may not be deemed as an effective or even a satisfactory treatment. So there is still a reluctance to regard a walk in the countryside or participation in a green gym as having the same sort of therapeutic status as psychiatric medication or psychological therapies. Therefore, there is a credibility issue for both GPs and patients that needs to be addressed. However, the real question is what contribution green exercise can make to existing effective packages of health and social care, by offering a greater treatment choice. A combination of treatments might be the answer, with green exercise acting as a complimentary therapy combined with drugs or other psychological therapies, rather than replacing them. Equally important is the contribution green exercise can make to a public health strategy for mental well-being that prevents people developing problems in the first place.

The benefits of green exercise should be promoted by public health campaigns to raise awareness. Usually they are launched in response to health crises and to discourage harmful activities (e.g. smoking), but they also have a role in promoting beneficial activities. Therefore, there is an opportunity for the health sectors to work with rural and urban regeneration agencies to promote the benefits of active engagement with the natural world as a key public health issue.

Those involved in hospital design and planning should also consider the value to patients and visitors of pleasant views from windows, of landscape artwork in wards and of hospital gardens. All patients in mental health inpatient facilities should have access to green space and opportunities for exercise.

Access and recreation providers

We need both more quality green spaces (especially in very urbanised areas) and to actively protect and conserve existing green spaces in both rural and urban locations. There seems to be a distinct incongruity between the benefits of green exercise and the existing drivers of economic development in both rural and urban areas. In the regeneration of urban areas green spaces are often ignored to minimise maintenance costs and private sector housing developments build as many homes as possible to take advantage of housing markets. The perception that well-vegetated places offer more opportunities for criminals and drug-dealers to hide remains a ubiquitous belief. In rural areas, modern agricultural development and the need for new housing continue to put pressure on green spaces where people can enjoy green exercise opportunities. A more sustainable holistic approach to land-use and planning is needed to maximise the full potential of green spaces for public services.

The extensive amount of accessible green space already available to the public constitutes a very significant health resource. However, too few people make use of these opportunities, access is unequally distributed and social exclusion is still problematic. Those social groups who could benefit most from contact with green spaces are least likely to access it. Groups with low participation rates in countryside recreation as a whole are young people, low-income groups, ethnic minorities and people with physical disabilities.

The challenge is to develop, manage and promote green spaces in ways that engage groups with low participation rates, attract socially excluded groups and meet the green space needs of new communities. We need to encourage access and recreation providers to ensure that more people have easy access to green areas within a short distance from their home, as this is a well-known factor in levels of exercise participation.

Access and recreation providers need to provide rights of way signage, promote their facilities and provide information of walking and cycling trails to encourage access and address perceptions of safety. They need to provide sustainable transport systems to connect people in urban areas with both nearby and remote countryside areas. Bus companies should be encouraged to provide bike carriers and look at prohibitive transport costs, especially for those communities experiencing the greatest 'poverty of place'.

Agricultural managers, environmental managers and policy makers

Agricultural managers and policy makers need to recognise the multifunctionality of our green spaces and reflect this in their policy and practice. Agencies with responsibility for maintaining our natural environment must take a lead role in promoting such an integrated and holistic approach. Managers of public green spaces need to increase use by forming partnerships with health agencies and local communities to raise awareness of the potential health benefits and attract new visitors. The farming industry needs to be encouraged to promote the opportunities for public health provision that land management can involve. Government should ensure that access ways provided by farmers are well maintained and connected up on a landscape scale.

Local and national Biodiversity Action Plans should be rewritten to include a component on biodiversity activities that contribute to public health. A good quality countryside or green space increases the value of the green exercise experience. Biodiversity is an important component of this quality and should be seen as a community service.

Planners and developers

Planners and developers should take account of the vital role that local green spaces or nearby nature plays for all people, and regard green space provision as part of future economic regeneration and new development strategies in both rural and urban areas. For example, Natural England's Accessible Natural Green Space Standards requires that no one should live more than 300m from their nearest green space of at least two hectares in size.

Planners and local authorities should therefore work closely with land managers to ensure that all communities, especially new ones on both green and brown field sites, have good quality, accessible and local green spaces (e.g. countryside, urban parks, country parks, allotments, urban farms and community gardens) within walking distance.

The impoverished environments that result from exaggerated concerns about crime (e.g. straight roads, bright lighting and removal of trees and other vegetation) are not good for mental well-being and, perversely, could even foster antisocial behaviour. Design for mental well-being should be as high a priority for planners and designers as designing against crime. For example, major developments such as the Thames Gateway and construction work for the 2012 Olympics provide excellent opportunities to develop practice in this area. The challenge is to deliver public and residential developments that take a holistic approach to design, incorporate green space and contribute to a public health policy for mental well-being (Mind 2007).

Social services

Social services should acknowledge that green exercise has clear mental health benefits, particularly for people engage as part of existing groups (e.g. families), or new groups (e.g. Walking the Way to Health, adventure therapy). Therefore, countryside agencies and local authorities should ensure their provision of services at recreation and leisure locations is focused on encouraging families and other groups. Crime and social service agencies should consider the therapeutic value of green exercise as part of strategies to address anti-social behaviour amongst adolescents.

Agencies responsible for providing social care services would also benefit from recognising the potential of green care and green exercise activities to increase the health and mental well-being of patients and clients. In the same way, the prison service, once well-renowned for recognising the benefits to inmates of working on a prison farm or garden, should consider extending this provision given its potential for making a happier, calmer and more socially adjusted prison population.

Probation services in some areas of the UK are already recognising the potential in Care Farming and horticultural projects to provide natural, green environments to deliver both mental health and employment dividends to ex-offenders. In times with increasing prison populations, a prevalence of prisoners with mental health problems and concerns over the effectiveness of current probation services, there is great potential for green exercise activities and green care to be used as an additional option in the rehabilitation of offenders.

Schools

Children now have less contact with nature and less opportunity to engage in informal creative play outdoors than ever before. Young people are becoming more disconnected from nature and they are making fewer visits to the countryside and urban parks. This is primarily due to parental safety fears, increasing road traffic and the attraction of indoor electronic entertainments. Consequently, their physical health, psychological well-being, social and cognitive development is being impaired.

Society is experiencing a "lost generation" of children and we need to build a movement to reconnect children to nature so that they can create memories, and develop their identity and sense of place. The value of summer camps, forest schools and school playing fields needs to be acknowledged. We need to encourage children to spend at least 25% of their time in the natural environment, compared to the mere 9% they spend at the moment.

If we can engage children with nature at a young age, this will encourage participation in outdoor exercise in later life. Therefore, schools should ensure that all primary age children experience visits to a range of types of countryside, woodlands, urban green space and farmland, and where possible establish their own on-site gardens and develop appropriate local sourcing for food for school meals. The Year of Food and Farming 2007 went some way in promoting the elements of healthy lifestyles and food and enabling children to visit farms and the wider countryside. Schools should also emphasise the public health value of physical activity for all children in the open air both through informal walking and cycling as well as formal sports.

Sports and leisure

The formal sports sector, from local to national level, should emphasise the health value of involvement in sports, as participation in some sports (e.g. football, cricket) is from a wider range of social groups than is countryside recreation. Gyms and fitness centres should improve the green aspects of their facilities (e.g. windows with green views, landscape pictures, television programmes). Strategic planning for promotion of a wide range of both formal and informal recreation activities should be encouraged.

Working in partnership

It is clear that green exercise has implications for many sectors, suggesting the need for cross-disciplinary and cross-sectoral strategies and action. The majority of countryside visits are informal, and so countryside agencies should consider how better to market the countryside as a health resource to a wide range of social groups and encourage land managers and farmers to advertise the health benefits of their resources.

Health agencies should advertise the mental health benefits of physical activities in rural and urban green spaces and the private sector, particularly the food manufacture and retail industry, could be engaged in partnerships for provision of both healthy food and healthy places where the food is raised and grown. All public and private agencies should consider the value to the mental health and well-being of employees and customers of a pleasant outdoor landscape, water, indoor vegetation and fresh flowers, nature posters and paintings, which all can be readily incorporated into the local physical environment with minimal expense.

Often research institutions face problems in accessing people to engage in their research, which is vital in developing the evidence base. Therefore encouraging academic institutions, the health sector and pubic and private companies to work in partnership will help to inform policy decisions.

2.5 Conclusions

If green exercise can have such a positive effect on health, why are more people not regularly taking exercise and visiting green spaces? Firstly, it is apparent from current participation rates that a large proportion of the UK population do already engage in various forms of green exercise, even it if it not always recognised as such. Thus, there is already a health dividend being experienced, but it is the reasonably healthy groups that are utilising it the most. Recent data indicate that a substantial proportion of the population is in danger of becoming obese and too sedentary and we still need to do a lot more to engage this part of the population, and other social groups not currently using green spaces. It is clear that there are barriers to participation, which affect different groups of people in different ways, and a key challenge for environmental and health policy is to find ways to remove these barriers to participation. The rise in inactivity levels and the associated problems with obesity are a priority on the government's agenda and, although there is a general acknowledgement that green spaces encourage physical activity, the relationship needs further investigation to develop a deeper understanding.

We need to change people's behaviour forever by creating sustainable lifestyles rather than just introducing a quick fix. Participating in physical activities in outdoor green environments seems to be a more sustainable option in maintaining long-term activity levels. It is the interaction with the environment and the social contact that are the main incentives for people to take part in green exercise and the health benefits derived from the exercise are secondary reasons (see Chapter 3). Well-managed, high quality, accessible green spaces are essential for long-term sustainability and healthy communities. Green spaces offer collective benefits for which there are no proxies, so they warrant investment, but we do need to conduct full economic valuation of these benefits. An economic study could highlight the potential savings for the NHS, add further credence to the argument, attract national interest and be used to set objectives for policy development.

To conclude, green exercise seems to be effective in generating a variety of physical and mental health benefits and fostering social bonds, which leads to healthier communities and reduces public health costs. It also contributes to the argument for protecting and conserving our natural resources (both countryside and urban green infrastructure). The positive outcomes of green exercise on health therefore have implications for direct intervention amongst people who are physically or mentally unwell (green care) and for the redesign of environments (buildings, gardens, urban areas or rural landscapes) so that people can be well (green design). In order to take advantage of these opportunities to increase the health and green space dividend, we still need a wide range of policy reform.

3

Practical Applications
of Green Space and Health

WILLIAM BIRD, NATURAL ENGLAND

3.1 Introduction

The Health Policy for Natural England includes a commitment to connect people to the natural environment[1], but why is this important? The policy says that it is important because 'biodiversity is valued more when connected to people and places', although perhaps this could be better phrased 'because people are valued more when connected to biodiversity and places'. Another key reason underpinning its importance is because the natural environment supports physical, mental and spiritual health and well-being.

Using psycho-physiological stress recovery theory, which is still a developing field, Roger Ulrich (Ulrich 1984) tells us that there is a part of our brain where there is a deep reflex, left there as a genetic imprint, so that when a person looks at nature their blood pressure immediately reduces and pulse rate decreases. This effect happens in minutes, which shows that much of this response is a reflex and is probably controlled in the most basic part of our brain, the limbic system, which is a kind of primitive brain. Nakamura and Fujii (1990) conducted a study in Japan where they used an electroencephalogram (EEG) to measure brain electrical activity while showing test subjects plant pots with and without foliage and flowers. The EEG showed that alpha rhythm activity, which show rest and a feeling of calm, were far more active when subjects were shown pots with foliage and flowers, less active when shown pots with foliage only and least active when shown pots with no foliage or flowers. They demonstrated a clear dose-response. They also repeated the study with a concrete wall, a hedge and a mixture of the two, with similar results.

There is something which resonates deep inside us and which results in our brain waves actually changing as we look at more natural scenes compared with artificial ones. We have no control over the response; it is a primitive reflex, probably present for evolutionary reasons. In earlier research (Ulrich 1981) it has been shown that even just looking at pictures of nature can lead to a reduction in blood pressure following a stressful event. The data clearly show that the blood pressure of the test subjects increased after they had been stressed but dropped much more rapidly when looking at pictures of nature compared to pictures of urban areas with traffic or a pedestrian shopping centre. Again, this is a reflex, a primitive brain response.

[1] Available from www.naturalengland.org.uk/ourwork/enjoying/health/ Accessed July 2009

3.2 The Individual Response

Concentration is the ability to prevent the brain focusing on things coming into your vision and into your hearing. Within the brain concentration is controlled by inhibitory fibres, which are nerve fibres that inhibit the activity of nerve cells. Concentration can only be maintained for a certain amount of time because inhibitory fibres get tired. If the inhibitory fibres are being constantly used, through overwork or not getting enough sleep, then people start to exhibit attributes such as irritability, compulsive behaviour or impulsive behaviour. Attention Restoration Theory (ART) proposes that natural environments, as they draw our attention but in an effortless way, serve to restore our ability to concentrate and direct attention to tasks that require more active attention. Attention restoration seems to be an important aspect of the response to green spaces and natural environments. It is suggested that our response to green spaces and natural environments occurs in the right frontal cortex of the brain, which is the area that controls non-verbal abilities such as memory, impulse control and problem solving.

There is a close correlation between brain attributes of children up to the age of eight with Attention Deficit Hyperactivity Disorder (ADHD) and those of people in areas of poverty. This is potentially because areas of poverty have fewer areas of green space. Mitchell and Popham (2008) also found that populations that are exposed to the greenest environments also have lowest levels of health inequality related to income deprivation. It has been shown on functional Magnetic Resonance Imaging (fMRI) scans that the same area of the brain is affected in children with ADHD and in people who are stressed.

Natural spaces and being in nature restores the functioning of this part of the brain more quickly than any other treatment. Being in green spaces also provides a deeper restoration that is more resilient to being re-stressed. Many studies have shown this response to be consistent; going out in nature is by far the best way to restore those inhibitory fibres and allow full concentration again. Investigations of many of the effects of being in nature are looking at this ART as the causal mechanism. However, it is still a theory and evidence is only slowly emerging as the effect is hard to measure, but it is a promising explanation.

In one Ulrich's first studies (Ulrich 1984) he looked at the recovery of patients in two different wards who had gall bladder surgery over a period of about six years. One ward window looked out onto the green trees, the other looked out onto a brick wall. The results of the study (see Figure 3-1) showed that those with a view of green trees needed less strong and less moderate analgesia compared to those who only had a view of a wall. There were also fewer negative comments in the medical notes of the group with a tree view and there was slight but significant reduction in length of stay.

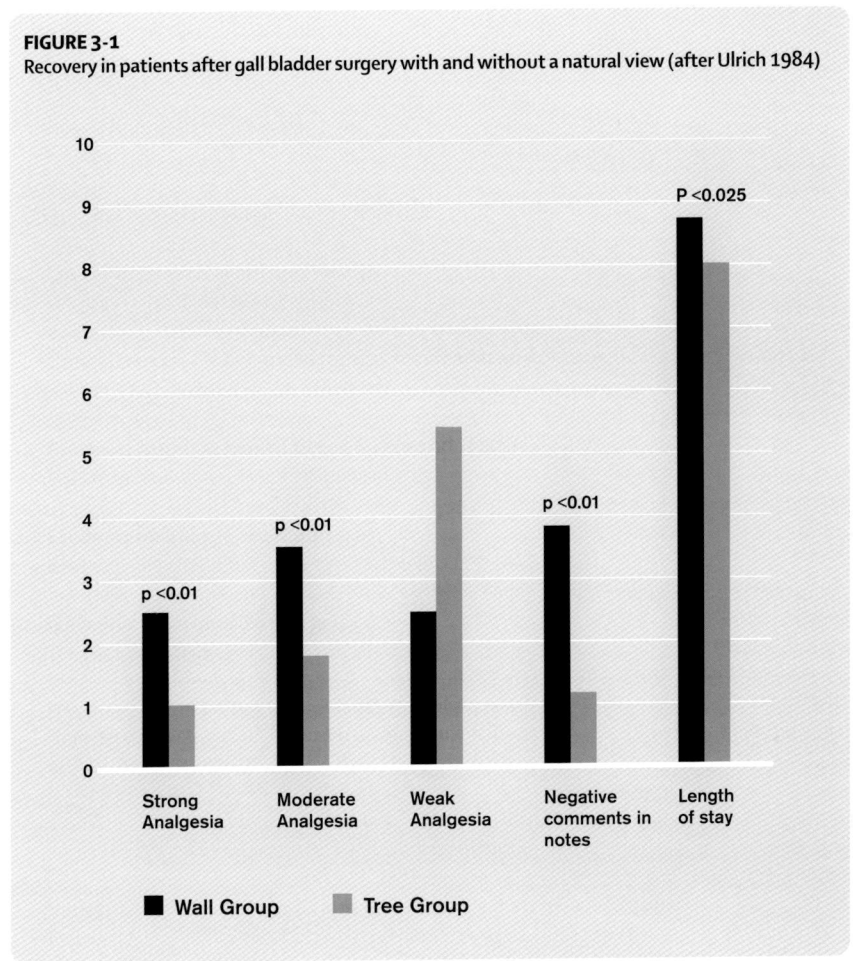

FIGURE 3-1
Recovery in patients after gall bladder surgery with and without a natural view (after Ulrich 1984)

This response can be explained by ART, which would suggest that patients with a green view cope better with the stress of being post operative. Studies looking at patients coping with cancer have found similar responses (e.g. Cimprich 1993). Also, it has been found that if bird song is played and the patient looks at nature during a broncoscopy they do not need as much anaesthetic and analgesia because that immediate sense of being in contact with nature reduces stress (Diette *et al.* 2003).

3.3 The Community Response

Moving from the individual to the community level these types of responses can also be seen. A study looking at different groups within the community of a housing project in Chicago (Coley *et al.* 1997), where some people had green open space and some just had concrete open spaces, found that people congregated and talked to each other far more where there was green open spaces. The only group that did not respond in this way were teenagers between the age of about 14 and 18. In this case, they appear to just listen to their peer groups and like to hang out in the urban part of the area and in shopping centres, but by the age of 19 or 20 they are congregating again in green spaces. Incorporating green spaces can therefore help to rebuild communities by getting people talking and interacting. Again, this could be the attention restoration effect making people feel much calmer.

FIGURE 3-2
People using open space around housing areas: The effect of green space.

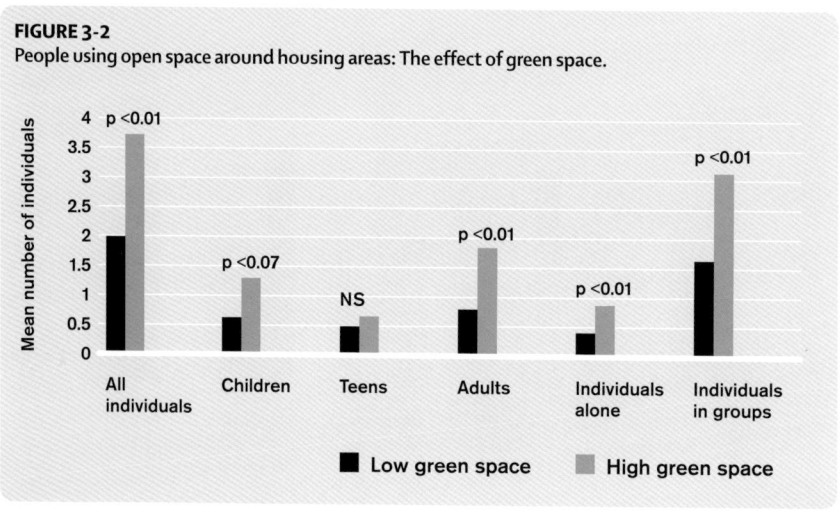

Another reason why it is good to connect people to the natural environment is that it creates environmentalists, people who understand about the natural environment and will evangelise about it, see a value in it, and preserve and work in it. Wells and Lekies (2006) interviewed 2000 adults in the US about their relationship with nature and found results that demonstrate the importance of early experiences with nature. These results are consistent with other studies that have looked into this effect. They found that there are three key predictors of lifelong positive environmental behaviour: contact with nature before the age of 11, that contact being with wild nature (i.e. not just gardens, although that can help), and being unsupervised for at least part of the time. So, getting children up to 11 years old involved with nature is vital to creating and maintaining a will to protect, enhance and value the environment. As well as making it more difficult to generate support for nature conservation as adults, children who do not get this early exposure to unsupervised wild nature have shown that they cannot use the natural environment to cope with stress as well as those who have had that exposure; it is simply not part of their make-up because nature is not valued. Those people who go out for a walk when they are stressed and can de-stress themselves in the natural environment are actually going back to what they have learnt earlier in life. Every year another group of children grow up past the age of 12 and the opportunity is lost to give them this advantage in life. We must somehow connect them with nature.

There are essentially two ways to address the challenge of reconnecting people with nature: increase the supply of green space and get more people into the green space that exists. Preferably both are done together. There is, however, a tendency to focus on the supply, particularly within environment-related organisations, but there is also a need to change behaviour to increase the demand for green spaces. Natural England's Accessible Natural Greenspace Standard (ANGSt) (see Harrison *et al.* 1995 and Land Use Consultants 2008) provide a set of benchmarks for ensuring access to green space, including a recommendation that people have an accessible natural green space of at least two hectares within 300 metres of where they live.

There are lots of barriers to parents letting their children out alone to explore green spaces. There is perception of a high risk of crime, kidnapping or stalkers, which has been exaggerated by the coverage given to crime in the media. Evidence that this view is widespread has come from a survey carried out by the Children's Society[2]. They found that when asked what parents thought is the best age for children to be allowed out with friends unsupervised, 43% of respondents said 14 or over, despite the fact that most of them had been allowed out without an adult at the much younger age of 10 or under. This unfortunately is past that critical 11–12 age group where attitudes to the environment can be set. If parents were aware that this is damaging their child, and that the evidence for this is very clear and very strong, then this may change views.

So why has this problem come about? We have all have a set of values. We value ourselves as individuals, we value our environment and we value our community, which can be thought of as where we work, our friends, and our family. For the last 10,000 years that man has been practising agriculture there has been a balance between those three things: the individual, the community and the environment, which probably has some genetically determined basis. We do not look after ourselves at the expense of the community; we do not look after our community without remembering ourselves and the environment. Then we became industrialised, the environment was not needed so much and our views became very human orientated, but our community was still important. In the last 60 years, we have begun to think that we do not even need our communities any more, and society has become much more individualistic. We are much more wealthy and we have lost the balance between those three elements.

[2] www.goodchildhood.org.uk

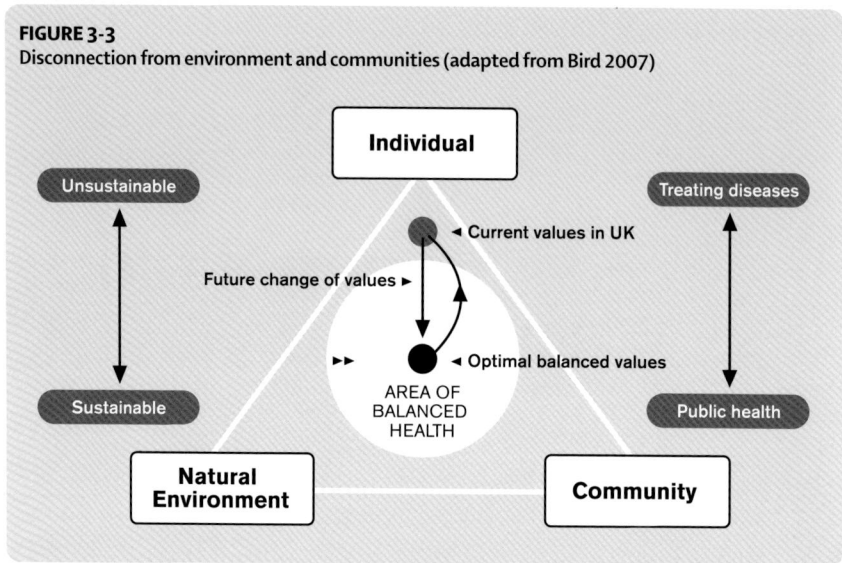

FIGURE 3-3
Disconnection from environment and communities (adapted from Bird 2007)

In moving from a state of balance between the environment, the community and the individual in those two stages there has been a progressive decrease in sustainability. Another important consequence of this is that we now have a National Health Service (NHS) which is disease driven at the level of individuals, because now only diseases are seen as important. Public health is, of course, taken into account but it is considered less important in a disease driven society that puts so much importance on the individual at the expense of the community. In these circumstances, public health is marginalised and the environment and community are forgotten. The challenge, therefore, is to incorporate the environment and community into health policy. It is important that both these elements are included; it will not work just incorporating environmental considerations. How people value society is just as important.

3.4 The Way Forward

Our current views of getting fit revolve predominantly around indoor exercise and our views of treating diseases revolve around clinical treatments and hospital interventions. The way to change these views are to present alternatives in terms of costs and show alternative, lower cost, ways of delivering NHS objectives. Figure 3-4 compares the healthcare costs for a population over the course of a lifetime when they are active and inactive. As the population ages these additional costs become much higher and by the age of 60 there is a very large gap between active and inactive groups.

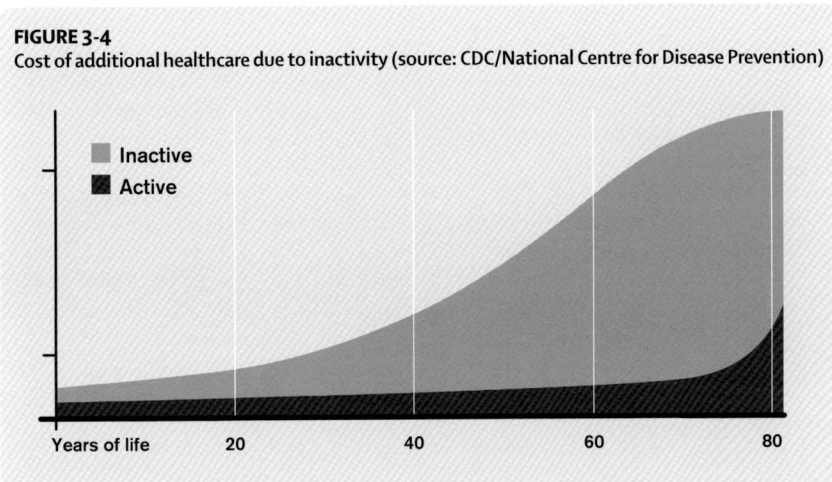

FIGURE 3-4
Cost of additional healthcare due to inactivity (source: CDC/National Centre for Disease Prevention)

The current policy emphasis is on sports, gyms and leisure centres. Politicians frequently talk about sport being a solution to health problems. Sport England carried out a survey (Sport England 2007) and, although the methodology tried to exclude all commuting and walking to get around, they found walking to be the exercise activity most people participated in (Figure 3-5). If walking for commuting is included then walking as a form of exercise becomes even more important.

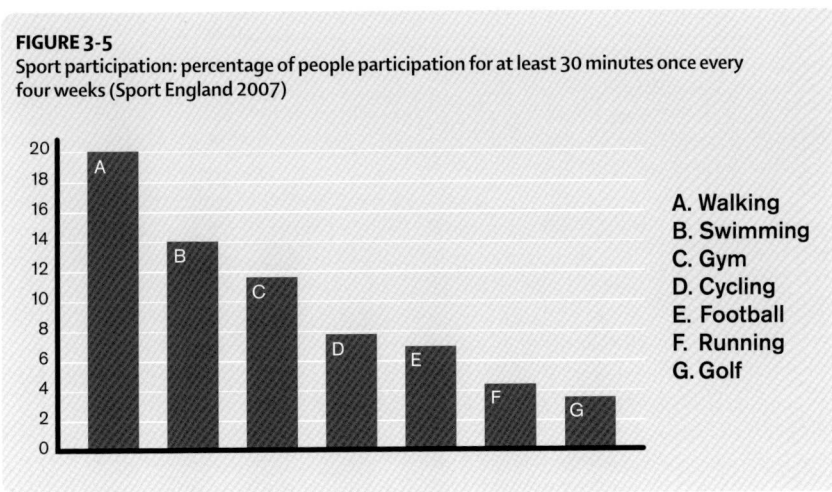

FIGURE 3-5
Sport participation: percentage of people participation for at least 30 minutes once every four weeks (Sport England 2007)

A. Walking
B. Swimming
C. Gym
D. Cycling
E. Football
F. Running
G. Golf

But other leisure activities, like gardening, were also excluded in this survey. Figure 3-6 shows physical activity in minutes per day by region and by activity type (Office for National Statistics 2000). It is clear that walking and gardening, the green exercises, account for the large majority of time spent in physical activity. Nevertheless, other activities receive the most government attention and funding.

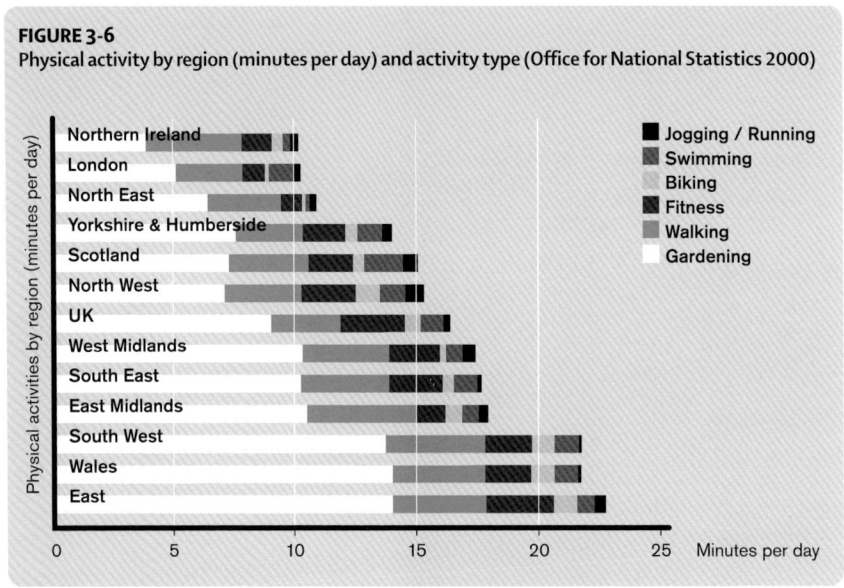

FIGURE 3-6
Physical activity by region (minutes per day) and activity type (Office for National Statistics 2000)

Although it has its place, sport is not the answer to encourage physical activity across the wider population. Green exercise is better at keeping people active for longer. If people go to a gym, there is about an 80% drop-out in six weeks. Ashley et al. (2000) looked at the reasons why people carry on doing health walks outside (Figure 3-7). Typically, the reasons a GP would give a patient to encourage them to be active would be that they would feel better, sleep better, and lose weight. In fact, Ashley et al. (2000) found that losing weight is not that important to people, and neither are health walks on their own a particularly effective way of losing weight. The most important reasons why people continued were improved fitness, being in the countryside, the fact that it was nearby and that it was enjoyable and fun. People also liked being able to watch the seasons go by. All of these reasons were more important than sleeping better, losing weight or the fact their GP told them. The health benefits may attract people in the first place to exercising but, by themselves, they will not encourage them to continue doing it.

Experiences from the Green Gym[3] have shown that the motivations of people to participate change over time. At the start, very consistently, 100% of Green Gym participants got involved because they felt they wanted to get fitter and improve their health. Fifty per cent of them wanted to join to be in the countryside. After six months, the health improvement was a much less important reason for continuing (about 45% cited this reason), but being in the countryside became much more important (about 75% cited this reason). So, again, health improvements can be used as a reason to get people involved, but on its own will not keep people involved. What will keep them involved is that connection with the natural environment.

FIGURE 3-7
Motivations for people to continue to participate in Health Walks (Ashley *et al*. 2000)

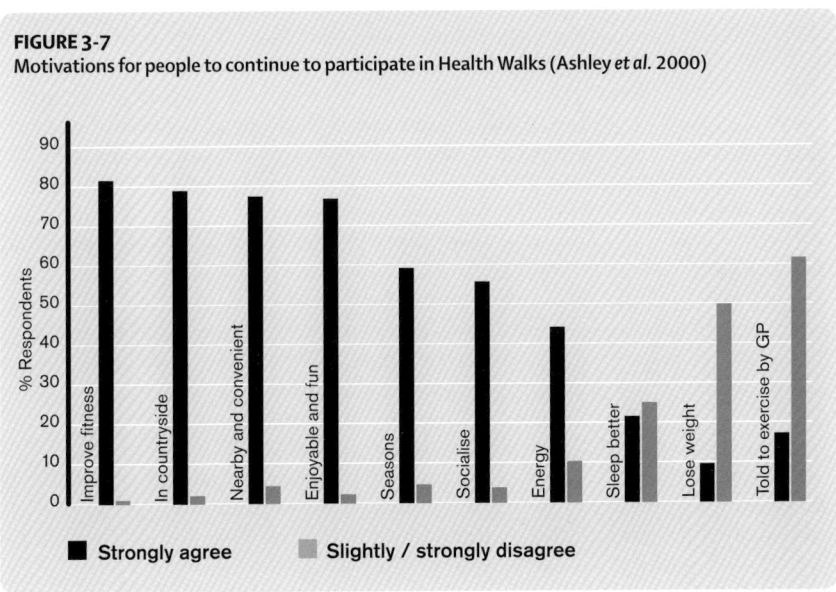

The evidence is clear, therefore, that activity in the natural environment improves people's health and well-being. The mechanisms involved can be elaborated by examining some individual conditions. The current budget for the NHS is £90 billion, and 10% of this is spent on diabetes. That is predicted to increase to 20% by 2020. About 1.3 million people in the UK have diagnosed diabetes and a further 1 million have undiagnosed diabetes. About 80% of diabetes is preventable by diet and exercise. For those at high risk, regular exercise reduces the chances of developing diabetes by 64% (DoH 2004b), so if we can get those high risk people, who are not unwell yet, to start exercising that would be an important means of reducing that future additional expenditure on diabetes.

[3] www.btcv.org.uk

Osteoarthritis affects 45% of people over 65 years old and is keeping more and more elderly people in nursing homes because they are unable to cope at home. It also has a significant effect on the pre-retirement age group with 36 million working days lost per year, costing £3.2 billion in lost earnings. Risk factors for developing osteoarthritis are being overweight and inactive, as it reduces muscle strength. Roddy et al. (2005) found that walking is as good as special strengthening exercise in reducing pain and increasing mobility. Hip and knee operations can also be delayed in those who already have osteoarthritis by doing physical activity.

The prevalence of Chronic Obstructive Pulmonary Disease (COPD), also known as emphysema, is continuing to increase, particularly in women. It affects 1% of the entire population and about 5–6% of the older population. Worldwide, it is projected to become one of the top three diseases, primarily because of smoking, particularly in developing countries. It will just be below AIDS and malaria in terms of mortality. Regular walking cut the admissions due to COPD by approximately 50% (Garcia-Aymerich et al. 2003). Admissions related to COPD cost the NHS £1 billion per year so there are potentially significant savings from encouraging increased activity. To illustrate this, let us assume we have 100 patients with COPD in a particular local area with a population of 10,000. Eight of those patients will be admitted to hospital because of their condition, usually in the winter. If these patients become physically active, either through a scheme or just on their own, the existing research shows us you can reduce admissions by about 50%, which would save the NHS about £10,000. If some of that money goes directly into local schemes to get people active then there is an immediate positive feedback effect.

There are many initiatives that are showing in practice how people can be encouraged to get out into the natural environment and the benefits that can be achieved. Natural England has been leading on the Walking the Way to Health scheme, which has been estimated to have encouraged more than a million people to walk more since 2000. One of the important aspects of these schemes is that they are locally sustained through either the NHS or local authorities. There are 536 schemes, with 37,000 people being trained up to be walk leaders[4]. That wide grassroots participation makes the scheme very influential, as there are now a large number of people active in their local communities who understand the connection between the natural environment and health and physical activity.

[4] www.whi.org.uk accessed July 2009

Phoenix House is working with drug rehabilitation and a study funded by Natural England has shown a 20% increase in retention in treatment amongst clients who take part in conservation therapy. This links to the ideas explored earlier regarding attention restoration theory. Drug rehabilitation is very stressful and with anything that involves stress, the natural environment can help to reduce it.

The Forestry Commission is also carrying out several practical projects related to the link between health and nature, such as the Forest Schools and Woodland Walks projects, plus many other evaluated schemes. The British Trust for Conservation Volunteers also have the Green Gyms programme for adults discussed above and there are plans for the Department of Health to provide money for Green Gyms in schools so children can take the option of conservation work or sport. There are many examples of local horticultural, gardening or conservation schemes, such as in Sydenham Gardens (Croydon) where a conservation scheme is attached to a GP practice. In addition there are the planners, architects, environmentalists and landowners who are all increasing the quality and quantity of green space locally.

The concept of a Natural Health Service is being developed in England (by Natural England) and Scotland to supplement the work of the NHS. This service will represent the green spaces surrounding health centres and hospitals. There are plans to create and NHS Forest in which 1.3 million trees will be planted, one for each NHS employee, to cool urban heat, provide shade, reduce stress and increase activity. The Department of Health has launched a physical activity plan in which the opportunities offered by the natural environment are central to getting the whole nation more active. A new scheme has been piloted by London GPs whereby patients are referred to parks and places for outdoor exercise. There are, therefore, many reasons to be optimistic.

Connecting people to the natural environment is important because biodiversity will be valued more and the biodiversity that is local to people will be protected. Having that connection will make people healthier, improve well-being and reduce health inequalities. So, by connecting people to the natural environment we are, in fact, valuing people more too. An increased connection will change people's behaviour towards the environment, but it is important to get children under the age of twelve engaged if we are going to maintain and increase this respect for the natural world in the future. To achieve this, we need to create and maintaining accessible green space and support programmes that get more people into that green space. If we connect with the natural environment and value it, then we will want to protect it and there will be a change to a culture of sustainable living, creating better and closer communities.

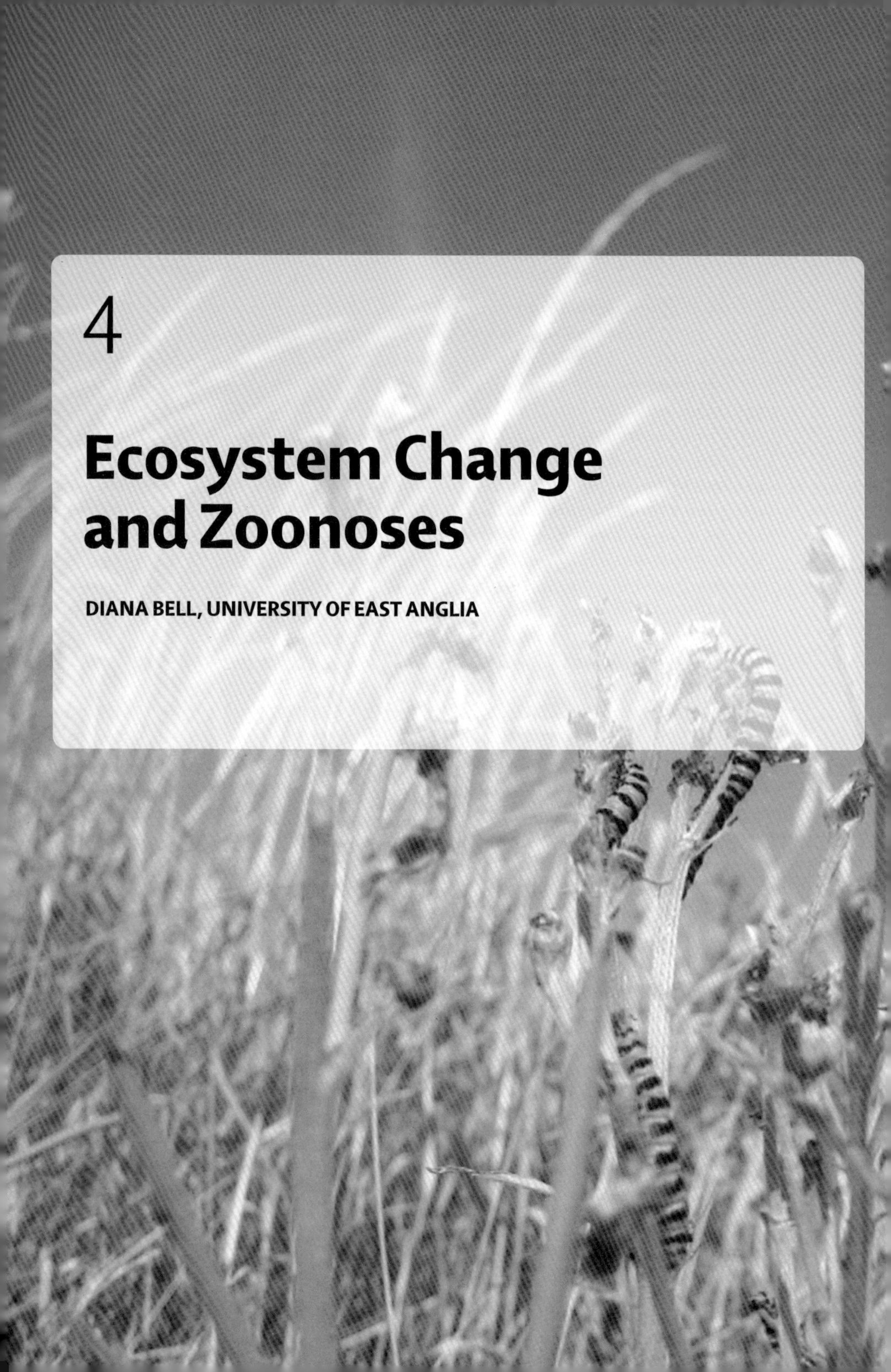

4

Ecosystem Change and Zoonoses

DIANA BELL, UNIVERSITY OF EAST ANGLIA

4.1 Introduction

Anthropogenic change to ecosystems as a consequence of expanding human populations, wildlife trade and a resulting increased frequency of human-wildlife contacts are the primary causes of both emerging zoonotic diseases (Chomel *et al.* 2007) and biodiversity loss (Bell *et al.* 2004). The potential impact of emerging infection epidemics on global economies and human livelihoods was vividly demonstrated by the consequences of severe acute respiratory syndrome (SARS) the first severe infectious disease to emerge in the twenty-first century. Research into the origins of this newly described coronavirus (SARS-CoV) also showed that the underlying roots of such emergent zoonotic diseases may lie in the parallel biodiversity crisis of species loss as a result of habitat destruction and human overexploitation of wild animal populations (Bell *et al.* 2004). This chapter firstly explores, with examples, the various ways in which the emergence of new zoonoses may be increased by anthropogenic ecosystem change and practices that promote human-wildlife contact. This will include consideration of habitat loss and alteration, changes in agricultural practice, climate change, introduced species, hunting and wildlife trade, ecotourism and exotic pet ownership. Secondly, it offers new approaches to assist in the prediction of future infectious diseases, and preventative measures that may help to combat these problems.

4.2 Deforestation, afforestation and agricultural change

Chomel *et al.* (2007) and Friend (1995) provide useful reviews of examples of diseases emerging under anthropogenic habitat alteration. These include the emergence and range expansion of Argentine haemorraghic fever in farm workers with the development of corn growing, which supports populations of the corn mouse, the primary reservoir host of the causal virus (Charrell and de Lamballerie 2003); the increased incidence of Lyme disease in humans with escalating deer populations and associated tick vectors with reafforestation in the USA; and Nipah virus in Malaysian pigs and humans due to a combination of deforestation and increased pig herds in association with fruit trees where the pigs became infected from virus-carrying fruit bats. During tropical forest removal, Daszak *et al.* (2004) suggest that the risks of disease emergence may be greater during selective logging than clear-felling due, for example, to the brief exposure to wildlife during the more rapid depopulation of animals in the latter. Furthermore, the movement of domestic species into deforested areas can have serious disease consequences for local wildlife. For example, there is exposure of naïve carnivore populations to canine distemper. Historically, the shift in agriculture to the Midwest from the eastern US allowed reforestation of New England and promoted environmental conditions favourable for Lyme disease (Daszak *et al.* 2000). Changing farming practices currently include a worldwide increase in deer farming, and their related tick borne pathogens, with New Zealand accounting for about 50% of the global population of farmed deer (Chomel *et al.* 2007).

Similarly, changes to intensive farming of domestic livestock can produce conditions in which pathogens, such as highly pathogenic avian influenzas including H5N1, may evolve and not attenuate due to the continuous availability of susceptible hosts.

It has been suggested that climate change related to anthropogenic activities is most likely to alter the ranges of vector-borne zoonotic diseases. For example, the risk of leishmaniasis becoming established in domestic dogs in the UK would be increased with elevated air temperatures required for the survival of Phelobotomus sand fly vectors (Fevre *et al.* 2006). Similarly, climate-related shifts in migratory ranges may alter the distribution of ectoparasite-borne pathogens in birds and mammals.

4.3 Wildlife and animal trade

In contrast to the import and export of live domestic animals, where information on the volume of different species is available for most countries from the Food and Agriculture Organisation (FAO), the extent of legal trade in wild animals is more difficult to quantify accurately despite various international and national monitoring and regulatory systems (see Cooper and Rosser 2002 and Fevre *et al.* 2006 for recent reviews and a range of examples where animal movements have introduced pathogens to areas which were previously disease-free). Furthermore, the extent of illegal movements of both domestic and wild animals across international borders can only be guessed at, usually from interception of consignments by various parties attempting to curtail this trade. However, accumulating evidence suggests that this illegal trade, in both animals and plants, is substantial (e.g. Bell *et al.* 2004; Karesh *et al.* 2005), ranking alongside the illegal drugs and arms trades in terms of the top three multi-billion dollar illegal activities. As several authors have observed (e.g. Fevre *et al.* 2006) the disease transmission risks of unregulated, illegally imported animals are greater because they bypass any regulatory veterinary procedures that are in place. This was demonstrated by the discovery of HPAI H5N1 in birds of prey illegally imported from Thailand which were intercepted at Antwerp airport (Van Borm *et al.* 2005) and of similarly infected birds imported for the UK pet trade (DEFRA 2005).

In live animal markets, or so-called wet markets, such as those found in SE Asia, the mixing of a wide variety of vertebrate species and populations which would not normally have had contact exacerbates cross-infection risks (Bell *et al.* 2004).

Although humans have hunted wildlife in tropical forests for many thousands of years many of the target species are now threatened with local and global extinction as a consequence of dramatic increases in hunting levels in recent decades (Milner-Gulland and Bennett 2002). These authors suggest that this pattern of overexploitation mirrors that of the rate of growth in human populations, forest loss and development; occurring first in Asia, is currently happening across Africa and is predicted for South America over the next 10–20 years. Other factors contributing to unsustainable levels of hunting include increased accessibility due to forest fragmentation and road building, loss of traditional hunting controls, developments in hunting technology, lack of alternative protein sources and long-distance transfer to urban markets where wild meat may be a preferred food or have alleged medicinal properties (Robinson and Bennett 2000). The resulting biodiversity loss not only has dramatic implications for tropical forest dynamics and ecosystem services (e.g. Fa *et al.* 2002), but the trade systems involved pose direct risks for emerging infectious diseases in animals and man (Bell *et al.* 2004; Swift *et al.* 2007).

In Lao PDR and Vietnam, for example, there has been a substantial increase in wildlife trade over the past 15 years, with the latter country playing a key role in supplying international demand for many species, particularly to China (Duckworth *et al.* 1999; Bell *et al.* 2004). Subsistence hunting appears to have been replaced by sale into the wildlife trade in Vietnam for a variety of species including civets, wild pig, deer, porcupine and snakes. The primary driver of this shift has been increased market prices and increasing affluence in the region (Roberton *et al.* 2006; Bell *et al.* 2004). We have previously highlighted (Bell *et al.* 2004) that this combination of events presents a suite of ecological conditions favourable for the emergence of new zoonotic diseases. These ecological shifts include:

1. The change from subsistence hunting to the sale of captured animals into an expanding wildlife trade

2. The extensive cross-exposure within this wildlife trade of species and species populations which would not mix or contact under natural conditions

3. The exploitation of new source populations and their pathogens and parasites as areas become depleted of target prey

4. The rapid movement of live animals, often over vast distances, through an expanding international wildlife trade network and to newly exposed, infection naïve human or animal consumer populations.

4.4 SARS

In the case of SARS Co-V, we had postulated that the source of this zoonotic virus was in the illegal, international trade in a range of wildlife taxa from SE Asia into China (Bell *et al.* 2004). Subsequent evidence in support of this hypothesis came from several sources (Bell *et al.* 2005). Firstly, significantly higher numbers of animal traders working in wildlife markets tested positive for SARS-CoV IgG antibodies than control groups employed in civet farms. Secondly, detailed analysis of the early epidemiology of the SARS epidemic in Guangdong (Xu *et al.* 2004) confirmed that a high percentage were categorised as 'food handlers' (i.e. prepared and served food or handled, killed and sold animals for food) although none were livestock or poultry farmers. Also, early-phase patients were more likely to live close to a market selling and/or killing live animals than late-phase cases. Of particular interest to us was the observation that the index patient in Guangxi province was a young man who worked as a driver for a wild animal dealer who 'supplied Guangdong market with wild animals from Guangxi, other Chinese provinces, and Vietnam'.

There is subsequent evidence that bats may be acting as a reservoir host for SARS-like coronaviruses in China (Li *et al.* 2005; Lau *et al.* 2005; Vijaykrishna *et al.* 2007) and may have infected civets in the animal markets in southern China, however a comparative sweep testing of all species in these trade systems would be required before bats can be identified as the causal reservoir. This should include pest species present in animal trade environments such as rodents, which may also act as a pathogen source or transmitter taxa.

Zoonotic diseases associated with the African wild meat trade include Ebola (Leroy *et al.* 2004; Rouquet *et al.* 2005), simian retrovirus infections (Wolfe et al. 2004), monkeypox (Jezek *et al.* 1986) and primate T-lymphotropic viruses (Wolfe *et al.* 2005). Simian immunodeficiency viruses (Hahn *et al.* 2000), for example, were detected in hunters following contact with or consumption of non-human primates (Chomel *et al.* 2007).

4.5 Pet trade, particularly exotic animals and travel

Recent changes in legislation allowing the international movements of pets on pet passports may increase the risk of importation into the UK of diseases and parasites such as echinococcosis (*Echinococcus multilocularis* and *E. granulosus*), babesiosis (*Babesia canis*), heart-worm (*Dirofilaria immitis*), ehrlichiosis (*Ehrlichia canis*) and *Leishmania infantum* (Fevre *et al.* 2006). The latter authors advocate the use of anthelminthics and deltamethrin-impregnated dog collars as preventative measures when pets are outside UK. Other existing recent examples of pet related human infections include Salmonella from reptiles (CDC 2003: Greene 2007) and African pygmy hedghogs (Riley and Chomel 2005), Hepatitis E infection of an owner by a pet pig in France (Renou *et al.* 2007) and B-virus from pet macaques in the USA (Ostrowski *et al.* 1998). Similarly monkeypox was recently imported into the USA via Gambian jumping rats which infected prairie dogs and their subsequent owners at a pet-swap (Reed *et al.* 2004; Reynolds *et al.* 2007; Chapter 5) while Leptospirosis was detected in pet traders exposed to southern flying squirrels imported from the USA to Japan (Masuzawa *et al.* 2006).

Ecotourism also brings people into close contact with wild animals and pathogen vectors, such as ungulate ticks, which transmit diseases such as African tick bite fever (Jensenius *et al.* 2003; Oostvogel *et al.* 2007). Such proximity can also cause the transmission of pathogens from human to wildlife, such as measles to mountain gorillas and poliovirus to chimpanzees in the wild (Dazsak *et al.* 2000). Recreational hunting similarly causes direct exposure of humans to pathogens carried by a variety of prey and examples include hepatitis E contracted by deer and boar hunters (Takahashi *et al.* 2004) and avian influenza among waterfowl hunters and wildlife professionals (Gill *et al.* 2006).

Many forms of international travel can also result in the importation of pathogens into new areas where competent vectors are present as occurred with the outbreak of Chikungunya in Italy in the late summer of 2007 (Promed 2007).

4.6 Introduced species

There are increasing numbers of examples of new infections appearing in native host taxa as a consequence of the accidental or deliberate introduction or natural range expansion of infected species. Examples include the well-documented spread by introduced taxa of a fungal disease in amphibians, chytridiomycosis, which has been identified as one of the major factors contributing to the current decline in frogs and toads worldwide (Berger *et al.* 1998; Daszak *et al.* 2000). Fevre *et al.* (2006) describe how the appearance of an opisthorchid fluke parasite into European otters in England has been associated with the escape into Hampshire rivers of the topmouth gudgeon (Pseudorasbora parva) and the sunbleak (Leucaspius delineatus), two non-native freshwater fishes that can act as intermediate hosts for the fluke.

Animal introductions or translocations may be for conservation purposes (to increase the range and population size of threatened taxa) or for a variety of other purposes including hunting or the import of exotic/domestic pet species and domestic livestock. A well-known example of the latter was the introduction in the late 1800s of a morbilivirus, Rinderpest, to Africa via cattle from Asia that depleting bovid populations and travelled 5000km in 10 years. Similarly, it is likely that brucellosis was introduced into America via cattle (Daszak *et al.* 2000). Other examples include an increase in reservoir hosts for rabies due the accidental release of animals farmed for fur, such as raccoon dogs (Nyctereutes procyonoides) in eastern Europe and the infection of customs officers with psittacosis through interception of illegally important parakeets (Chomel *et al.* 2007).

Similarly, rabies was introduced to the mid-Atlantic US states by a translocation of infected raccoons for hunting (Dazsak *et al.* 2000) and the distant transfer to abattoirs of infected pigs and cattle has translocated pathogens in the UK (Fevre *et al.* 2006). Canine distemper and rabies from sympatric domestic dogs is threatening the African wild dog.

We have recently highlighted the endangered Mauritius pink pigeon as a model species in which to study the impact of exotic pathogens introduced to the island by several pigeon and dove taxa (Bunbury *et al.* 2007a, 2007b, 2008a, 2008b; Gaspar da Silva *et al.* 2007). The pink pigeon has recovered from 12 to over 370 individuals in the wild by an integrated programme of habitat restoration, captive breeding, reintroduction and control of exotic predators. However, two parasitic protozoa, *Trichomonas gallinae* and *Leucocytozoon marchouxi*, appear to be limiting population recovery of the species. The former, for example, is prevalent in all five subpopulations of pink pigeons where it causes high mortality among squabs and was also found in all exotic columbid taxa tested (Bunbury *et al.* 2008a).

4.7 Combating new zoonoses

Whilst some remain sceptical about our ability to predict new zoonoses (Murphy 1998), others are optimistic that this can be achieved using an interdisciplinary approach which combines the expertise of virologists, wildlife biologists, disease ecologists, anthropologists, economists, geographers and medical professionals (e.g. Dazsak *et al*. 2000; Wolfe *et al*. 2005; Bell *et al*. 2004; Daszak *et al*. 2004; Jones *et al*. 2008).

In a review which identified that 868 of 1415 (61%) species of infectious organisms pathogenic to humans were zoonotic, Taylor et al. (2001) found that 132 of 175 (75%) of emerging pathogens are zoonotic and that viruses and protozoa are particularly likely to emerge (see also Dobson and Foufopoulos 2001). A recent analysis of the origins of 335 emerging human infectious disease (EID) between 1940 and 2004 (Jones *et al*. 2008) also found that not only were these mainly zoonoses (60%), but that the majority originated in wildlife (72%) and that the number of the latter was increasing significantly over time. However, in contrast to earlier authors, 54% of EID events were identified as caused by bacteria or rickettsia indicating significant numbers of drug-resistant microbes, whilst percentages caused by protozoa, fungi and helminths were 11%, 6% and 3% respectively. Globally, Jones *et al*. (2008) also identify emerging disease hotspots where new EIDs are most likely to appear. They report high risks of vector-borne and wildlife zoonotic events at lower latitude developing countries and found that the latter EIDs are significantly correlated with wildlife biodiversity. In contrast, zoonotic EID events that did not originate from wildlife hosts were predicted by latitude, human population growth and density. This important database analysis offers an opportunity for predictive modelling of where new human EIDs are likely to appear and thus where to direct surveillance effort, namely tropical Africa, Latin America and Asia. The important point is made that reducing human activity as a means of conserving biodiversity hotspots may also reduce emergence of future zoonotic disease.

Here, I suggest that an intercontinental comparison of wildlife trade systems may further help us to predict new zoonoses.

In areas of African tropical moist forest, meat from wild animals is a highly valued product by many rural and urban people and is an important source of protein for many households (Fa *et al*. 2005). In a comparative study, Fa *et al*. (2002) estimate that five million tonnes of wild mammal meat annually feeds millions of people in the Neotropical Amazon Basin (0.15 million tonnes) and Afrotropical Congo Basin (4.9 million tonnes) forests. Their calculated extraction rates were significantly lower in the former than the latter.

Harvest rates across the Congo Basin have increased beyond sustainable levels as a consequence of human population growth, increased demand from urban areas, increased access to forests via the spread of roads and a resulting increase in hunter numbers and more efficient hunting techniques (Fa *et al.* 2005). In contrast, wild meat extraction rates in the Amazon Basin are lower due to subsistence hunting and lower human population density, although road development into Amazonia has provided infrastructure for a wildlife trade system. Local consumption of hunted taxa is also less likely to result in the rapid spread of new zoonoses than in the long-distance movement of taxa to high density urban markets and new immunologically naïve hosts such as that found in SE Asia (Swift *et al.* 2007). One may predict that the rates of emerging zoonotic diseases of wildlife origin are, therefore, lower in Neotropical moist forests than those in SE Asian areas which have seen the shift from subsistence hunting to sale into international trade described earlier.

The species targeted for exploitation can also be compared across continents. In the African bushmeat trade, there has been a shift from large (ungulate) to small size mammals as populations are depleted (Fa *et al.* 2005), so one might predict an increase in the emergence of rodent related zoonotic diseases. Rodents only become significant prey taxa in disturbed areas in most continental African sites (Eves and Ruggiero 2000), indicating reduced availability of preferred wild meat species. In Amazonian forests, Peres (2000) and Jerozolimskia and Peres (2003) similarly found that larger prey taxa rapidly decline with increased hunting pressure. Such changes from a smaller number of large-bodied animals to a larger number of small-bodied taxa also have pathogen-risk consequences for the volumes of individuals handled by hunters and others in the hunter to consumer chain (Swift *et al.*2007).

It is possible that this size shift is less likely to occur in SE Asia because of the confounding factor of traded species selection on the basis of reputed medicinal qualities. For example, different taxa such as pangolins and civets are alleged to have specific medical properties, so substitution with alternative species may not be an option. However, the high densities of indiscriminate snare-traps set in Asian forests probably already includes the capture of large numbers of small-bodied mammals and there is also a reward scheme where people, often children, are paid specifically for each rat's tail they present in a rodent control campaign in Vietnam (S Roberton, pers. comm.).

Indeed, intercontinental comparative studies of hunting, transport, butchering and consumption of the carcasses are required, such as the anthropological research suggested by Dazsak et al. (2004). Important questions are, for example, are the animals transported live to markets (as in SE Asia) or are they butchered on capture or in the village, and by which demographic classes? Such studies should also explore taste preferences for particular taxa and those prized as luxury or popular food items by urban consumers. Any other reasons for taxa exploitation, such as use in local medicines, decorations or as pets, should also be distinguished. Comparative data on the availability of domestic livestock at study sites would also be valuable in determining the level of dependence on wild meat for food security or the relative attractiveness of wild versus domestic meats to consumers.

In regions such as Europe and North America, the primary threats of new wildlife zoonoses may be in the international pet trade, and the importation of taxa for hunting or for food or medicinal items for specific ethnic groups. Here, one may predict that the primary risks occur in small-bodied mammals and birds, which are popular because they are viewed as requiring less space and attention, although some of the disease risks documented for pet reptiles have already been mentioned. Chomel *et al.* (2007) report that hunting activities generate approximately 100,000 jobs in Europe, where there are an estimated 10 million hunters, and over 700, 000 jobs in the USA. A range of avian and mammalian taxa are imported for hunting purposes and, as examples mentioned earlier demonstrate, the handling and butchering of such animals exposes participants to parasites and any other pathogens they may be carrying.

On oceanic islands, imported pets, domestic livestock, insect vectors, translocated wildlife or exotic taxa imported as food are the most likely sources of new pathogens. Examples would include the arrival and spread to native amphibians of chytridiomycosis via anurans imported as food.

An obvious final recommendation would be to apply any knowledge we have gained from comparative analyses, such as that by Jones *et al.* (2008), to target disease surveillance effort more effectively. Most authors agree that surveillance systems should be improved at both national and international levels (Blancou *et al.* 2005; Chomel *et al.* 2007). This should include monitoring of vector ranges for arthropod-borne infectious diseases as a result of anthropogenic climate change (Dazsak *et al.* 2000).

On a local level, simply increasing the number of abattoirs in the UK would avoid long-distance movement of animals for slaughter, reducing the risk of long-range spread of any pathogens they may be carrying and have animal welfare benefits.

In high-risk regions, we need to increase the availability of protein from sources that minimise the evolution of highly pathogenic diseases by, for example, revising intensive farming practices and banning or imposing strict controls with deterrent penalties on wildlife trade. These cross-discipline issues require the complimentary expertise and approaches of international organisations and individuals, such as FAO, WHO, nutritionists, wildlife and conservation biologists, epidemiologists, veterinarians, social scientists, medical researchers and practitioners (Bell *et al.* 2004).

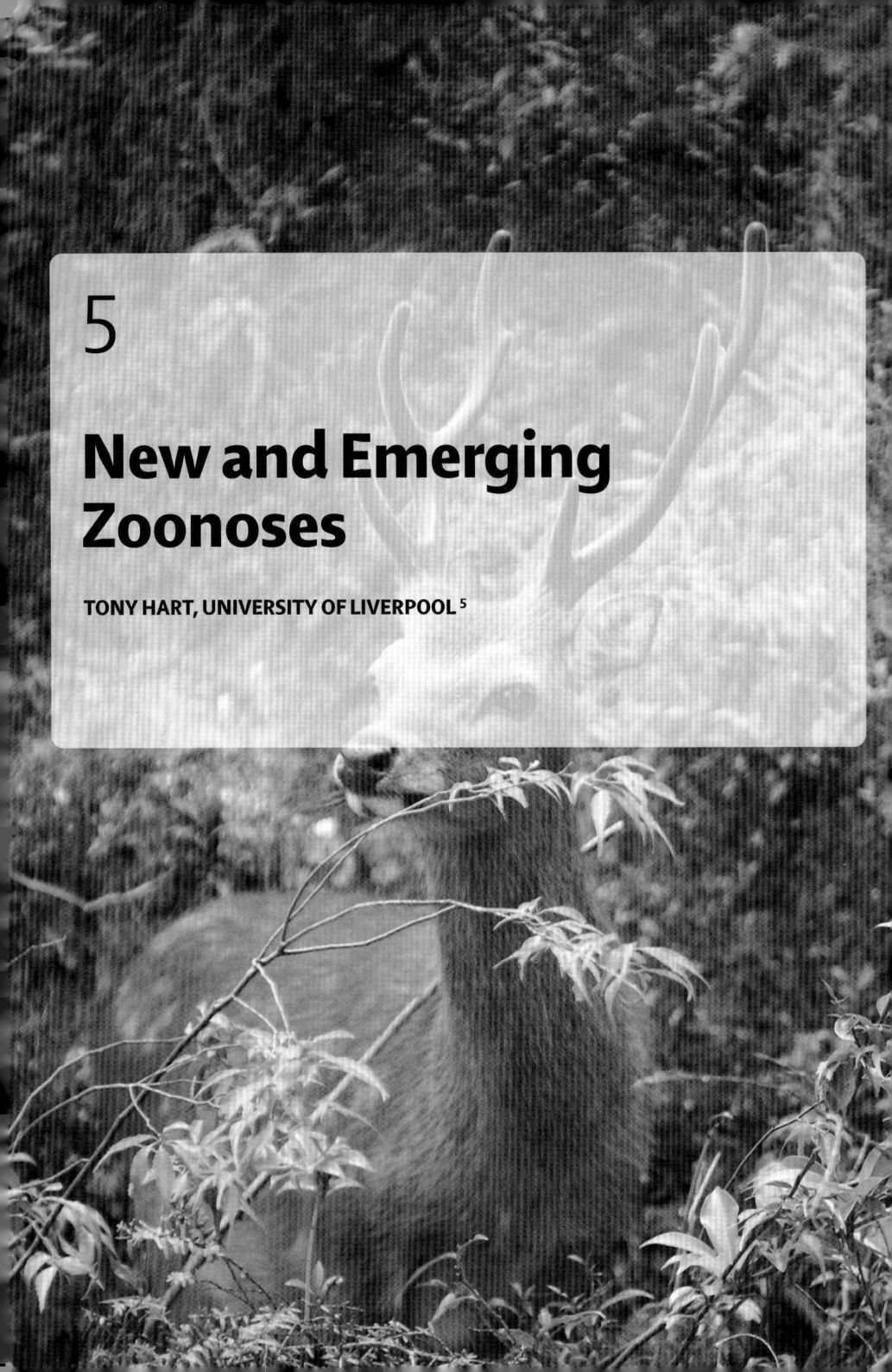

5

New and Emerging Zoonoses

TONY HART, UNIVERSITY OF LIVERPOOL [5]

5.1 Introduction

The term zoonosis was coined by Rudolph Virchow (1821–1902) and, after many years of disagreement, in 1959 it was accepted both by the FAO and the WHO. They defined it as those diseases and infections naturally transmitted between vertebrate animals and man. Of course, zoonoses predate this definition by quite a bit and were recognised in various early sources. In Deuteronomy 14 verse 8 it says, *'The swine because it divideth the hoof but cheweth not the cud shall be unclean to you'* and in Ezekiel 44 verse 13, *'Ye shall not eat anything that dieth of itself'*, presumably to prevent hydatids or other diseases spreading. But as you will see if you read on, Godliness is not at all next to neighbourliness: *'Thou shalt give it unto the stranger that is in thy gates, that he may eat it or thou mayest sell it unto an alien'*. So it's alright for some. Celsus in 100AD recognised that rabies may have come from animals and you have got to draw out the virus with a cupping glass, not very effective and quite painful but at least made the doctor feel better, which is what it is all about.

Researchers in the University of Edinburgh investigated how many different microorganisms there are that are pathogenic to humans and, after much effort, they counted about 1,870. Although 102 human parvoviruses were all included separately, it seems a surprisingly small number of things that can cause disease in people. One interesting aspect of these 1,870 pathogens is that 560 have emerged in the last 30 years and, of those 560, between two thirds and three quarters are zoonoses. So, most of the new infections that have been identified in humans are zoonoses. Looking at new infectious diseases that have emerged since 1973 (Figure 5-1), most of the ones identified from the 1990s onwards are zoonoses.

[5] Professor Tony Hart sadly passed away shortly after giving this paper at the Sibthorp Trust workshop. This paper has been written by the editors based on a transcribed audio recording of the presentation made by Tony and any errors or omissions are solely attributable to the editors.

FIGURE 5-1
Zoonoses emerging since 1973

1973	Rotavirus		1990	Human herpesvirus 7
1975	Human Parvovirus		1990	Hepatitis E virus
1975	Tanapoxvirus		1991	Guanarito virus
1975	Lassa virus		1992	*Vibrio cholerae* 0139
1976	Monkeypoxvirus		1992	*Rickettsia felis*
1976	Calicivirus		1992	Enteroaggegative *E. coli*
1976	*Cryptosporidium parvum*		1992	*Enterocytozoon bieneusii*
1977	*Clostridium difficile*		1992	*Campylobacter upsaliensis*
1977	Ebola virus		1992	*Baronella henselae*
1977	Flexal virus		1993	Sin Nombre virus
1977	*Legionella pneumophila*		1993	*Neisseria weaveri*
1977	Hepatitis D virus		1993	*Baylisascaris procyonis*
1977	*Campylobacter jejuni*		1993	*Simkania negevensis*
1980	Enteropathogen *E. coli*		1993	*Trophyrema whippelii*
1980	Astrovirus		1993	Human granulocytic ehrilichiosis
1980	HTLV-1		1994	Sabia virus
1980	*Haemophilus ducreyi*		1994	Hendra virus
1982	E. coli 0157		1995	Hepatitis G virus
1982	HTLV-2		1995	Human herpes virus 8
1982	*Borrelia burgdorferi*		1996	Whitewater Aroyo virus
1983	HIV-1		1996	Australian bat lyssavirus
1983	*Mobiluncus spp.*		1996	Varian CJD
1983	*Helicobacter pylori*		1996	Tulan virus
1983	Adenovirus 40/41		1997	Laguna Negra virus
1984	*Capnocytophaga canimorsus*		1997	Andes virus
1985	*Rhodococcus equi*		1997	Manangle virus
1985	HIV-2		1997	TTV
1985	Birnavirus		1998	Enterovirus 71 / Coxsackie chimera
1985	*Vibrio vulnificans*		1998	Nipah virus
1985	*Chlamydophila pneumoniae*		1998	Human Torovirus
1986	*Strongyloides fullebornii*		1999	SEN virus
1986	*Cyclospora cayetanensis*		2001	Human metapneumovirus
1988	Human herpesvirus-6		2002	Bermejo virus
1989	*Ehrlichia chaffeensis*		2002	*Burkholderia anthina*
1989	Hepatitis C virus		2002	*Inquilinus limosus*
1989	Human pestivirus		2003	SARS coronavirus

5.2 Classification of zoonoses

There are a number of possible ways to classify zoonoses, each with their own problems. They can be classified by:

- Animal species of origin
- Animal disease syndrome
- Human disease syndrome
- Mode of transmission
- Route of entry
- Pathogenic micro-organism
- Mode of acquisition

If zoonoses are classified by animal disease syndrome, the problem is that most of the zoonotic diseases cause no disease at all in the animal host, so it would not necessarily be known that it was there. Classification by animal species of origin is also problematic as patients do not always recall being in contact with animals and several species may harbour the same pathogen. The difficultly in classifying by human disease syndrome is that when doctors are presented with somebody who is ill it is difficult to identify whether it is a zoonosis or not. Often a zoonotic cause is the last option a doctor will consider when a patient has meningitis, or a fever, or a chest infection, so it may not be correctly diagnosed. As a result, it is very difficult to get accurate figures on zoonotic infections.

Classification by mode of transmissions or route of entry is possible, but many people will not know what has happened to give them their disease. Finally, zoonoses can be classified by pathogenic microorganism, but that is not particularly useful because salmonella, for example *S. typhimurium*, can be transmitted from animal to human, but it can also go from person to person, so it does not necessarily help as a classification method.

Considering mode of acquisition, the most likely modes of acquisition that could occur are through direct contact (through a scratch, abrasion or mucous membrane or from an animal bite), via arthropod vectors, via a respiratory route, by ingestion (such as faeco-oral contamination or ingestion of meat, fish, shellfish, eggs or dairy products). So, for example, a virus like rabies is transmitted by direct contact through a bite or even through a scratch if there was saliva put on it. A zoonosis could also be caused by an arthropod vector or through inhalation, by ingestion of food or water contaminated with animal faeces, ingestion of meat, fish or shellfish or even milk that is contaminated during production.

One other practical means of classification that is useful, in that it encourages consideration of how zoonoses may have emerged, is by classification into old zoonoses, recent zoonoses, established zoonoses, new and emerging zoonoses, and parazoonoses.

The old zoonoses are the infectious diseases that we have at present, the human ones. These are the epidemic and endemic human-specific infections that either evolved with us or were acquired by us very early in our evolutionary history. A good example is measles, which may or may not have come from rinderpest or canine distemper virus many years ago. But this only happened when mankind had big enough populations to support the transmission. There had to have been more than 10,000 people in the population before measles could be established and be maintained as a natural infection.

The recent zoonoses are the new or emerging human epidemic infections with a recent non-human source. These are diseases that move from person to person. Perhaps one of the most recent ones would be the human immunodeficiency virus (HIV). HIV-1 is now known to have come from a particular troop of chimpanzees found in Rwanda from simian immunodeficiency virus 1 (SIV-1). HIV-2 comes from SIV-2, which is found naturally in macaques. So, these have moved from animals to humans, but have only become established in people recently. The established zoonoses are all the classical ones in which are known to be transmitted from animal to human but the transmission from human to human is quite poor, so it is not very efficient in its transmission. Examples are rabies, the various cancer viruses, including the new ones found in the Americas, and Leptospirosis.

The new and emerging zoonoses, for example Ebola, Hendra and Nipah generate a lot of attention. These diseases have a non-human reservoir host, but have only recently been observed to spread to man. These diseases have almost certainly occurred in man before, but were not identified as zoonoses and can only now be diagnosed because of improved tools.

Finally, there are parazoonoses, which are infectious diseases epidemic or endemic in man, which change their virulence following acquisition of genes from non-human pathogens. It is not the organism that is of importance, but the genome of the pathogen. A recent high profile example of this is H5N1 influenza, which has its origin in birds but which is mutating and which may pick up other genes from other influenza viruses. Parazoonoses also include rotaviruses. Rotaviruses cause the deaths of between 400,000 and 600,000 children under five each year, principally in developing countries, by causing diarrhoeal disease. Rotaviruses are a fragmented genome virus with eleven segments of double stranded RNA that can cross species barriers, with the result that dog-human, cow-human, cat-human, chimeric rotaviruses are now found where different rotaviruses have infected one host species at the same time and there has been gene transfer.

Noroviruses, which cause gastroenteritis and spread easily as an aerosol, can also be considered to be a parazoonosis. It was thought noroviruses were solely human pathogens, but in fact there have now been large cats in zoos found to be infected with human noroviruses and cattle infected with cattle-human chimeric noroviruses. The hepatitis E virus, another parazoonosis, causes epidemics of food borne hepatitis. It is clinically similar to hepatitis A, except in the case of pregnant women, where it has about a 30% mortality rate. It also now appears that hepatitis E can also be acquired in Britain, previously it was always imported. Pigs have been found with the hepatitis E virus and there have been cases of transfers from pigs to humans.

Misuse of antibiotics can also give rise to genetic changes in microbes that lead to antimicrobial resistance. Vets were heavily criticised for being responsible for the emergence of antimicrobial resistance in the 1990s but, in fact, they have very carefully controlled antimicrobial usage and most of the resistance now is arising from residues of previous treatments or human misuse of antimicrobials. Antimicrobial resistance is not just an issue for domesticated animals; there are also links to the environment. Gilliver *et al.* (1999) conducted a research project where bank voles and wood mice were trapped, marked, released and trapped again. Their intestinal contents were sampled and the normal bacteria that live in them were extracted from it. These bacteria were tested to see if they were resistant to antibiotics or not and, surprisingly, significant antimicrobial resistance was found. These bank voles and wood mice would never have been in contact with antibiotics, so how have they acquired resistance? The likely answer is that the bacteria plasmids, which are extra-chromosomal DNA, carry a range of antibiotic resistant genes, but also mercury resistance. High levels of mercury were found when the soil at the study site was tested. It is suspected that the grain the wood mice were eating had high mercury levels and the intestinal bacteria in the wood mice were selected for those that had mercury resistance, but these also had these other antimicrobial resistances as well. This is another example of DNA that might then move to human pathogens.

As well as emerging zoonoses, we have re-emerging zoonoses, for example, Congo-Crimean Haemorrhagic Fever. This is spread by ticks, but also from person to person and is spreading between the Congo and Crimea. There is also Japanese encephalitis, which first emerged in 1867 and now has four different clones spread out all over south East Asia.

The human pox viruses, the most infamous of which is smallpox, spread with great ease and have a high mortality rate. Smallpox, for example, has about a 50% mortality rate. Monkeypox is very closely related to smallpox and is found in West Africa. It is zoonotic, although has also recently been observed to move from person to person, and causes epidemics in the tribal areas of the Democratic Republic of Congo. It is indistinguishable from smallpox clinically except the mortality rate is lower, at about 10%. The term monkeypox is a misnomer because monkeys are accidental hosts just like people are; the reservoir is small rodents, such as ground squirrels.

In 2003, an outbreak of monkeypox occurred in the US when a pet importer imported infected giant Gambian rats from West Africa. The rats were held in a pet holding facility near to Chicago along with prairie dogs, rabbits and a number of other species. The prairie dogs caught the virus and were subsequently taken to pet markets and sold across several states of the US. Many of the pet owners then became infected with monkeypox. Approximately 90 people were infected but none died, because it appears that this was a less virulent strain of monkeypox than some of the strains in Africa. There is now some concern whether it has moved from Africa and has become enzoootic in North America, given that giant Gambian rats, prairie dogs, a rabbit and several other pets that were held in the same facility had the virus and any of them may have escaped.

5.3 The UK context

Most of the zoonoses that have a major impact in the UK are food borne. The most frequent zoonoses are *Campylobacteriosis, Salmonellosis, Cryptosporidiosis* and *E coli* 0157, although the numbers of cases are not very great. All of these are acquired by ingestion. Part of the problem in understanding them as zoonoses is that they also move from person to person and in addition, for example with *Cryptosporidium*, there are human-specific strains and animal-specific strains. Probably of most concern is *Campylobacter*. In America, the incidence of infection is about 12.6 per 100,000 people per year, in England and Wales in the four years since 1996, there were almost 170,000 cases. That resulted in just short of 16,000 hospitalisations, about 60,000 hospital days and 80 deaths, so it has a major impact. Another survey that was carried out in England and Wales in 2001 found that there were 56,000 cases recorded, but this is probably a tenfold under estimate, given the limitations in recording. There are, therefore, approximately half a million cases each year in England and Wales. The most important of the *Campylobacter spp.* is *Campylobacter jejuni*, with approximately three quarters of cases of campylobacteriosis, then *Campylobacter coli* with 10–15% of cases and then *C. upsaliensis* and *C. lari. Campylobacter* illustrate the problem of the classification of zoonoses very well, it is carried silently in a wide variety of different animals, it can persist for long periods in the water environment and it is faeco-oral spread but it is rarely direct, typically being spread indirectly in food, water etc. The main route of transfer and the main reservoirs are not entirely clear, it is thought that it is mainly poultry, but it may not be. Other reservoirs include cattle, pigs, companion animals, wild mammals and wild birds, with different hosts having different *Campylobacter* species. Wild mammals and birds are host to a wide diversity of different *Campylobacter,* some of which are known to infect humans and some of which are newly identified. To illustrate the problem with poultry, in the big poultry houses *Campylobacter* are rarely detected before day 7 of the breeding cycle, but up to 100% of birds and 90–100% of flocks become carriers just before slaughter, predominantly with *Campylobacteria jejuni*. A study in England where 1515 cattle were screened found that 50.4% of the cattle were carrying *Campylobacter* demonstrating that cattle are an important reservoir too. Of those with *Campylobacter, C. jejuni* were found in 46.9% of cases, *C. coli* in 6%, and *C. lari* in 0.2%. Preventing transmission is, therefore, clearly a challenge.

Avian influenza
Variant CJD
Anaplasmosis
European bat lyssavirus
Babesiosis
Hantaviruses
Anthrax
Q-fever
Brucellosis

The key emerging or resurgent zoonoses of concern at the moment are shown in Box 5-1. Of these, avian influenza is probably of most concern to the public, and not just H5N1 as was seen with the outbreaks in England, there are other serious types of influenza that can cause disease.

Q-fever is caused by infection by the bacterium *Coxiella burnetii* and is highly infectious. In 2006 there was an epidemic of Q-fever in Glasgow caused by a pregnant sheep that aborted in an abattoir. This happened very close to the restaurant used by the abattoir workers. The aerosolled virus was carried by the air into the restaurant and some of the workers were infected.

Hantaviruses are also an increasing problem. There are two major forms of hantaviruses: those that cause haemorrhagic fever (bleeding into the skin) and those that infect the lungs. These are another good example of how the environment affects disease. The first case of a New World hantavirus occurred in a person who was exploring some caves in the Four Corners region of America (where New Mexico, Arizona, Colorado, and Utah abut in the south west of the US). He became ill with a flu-like illness, his lungs filled with fluid and he contracted terrible pneumonia and died. The medical examiner suspected that this was a new disease and sent samples to the Centre for Disease Control. Within six months they had identified the cause as a new type of hantavirus. Naming the new virus caused a problem. The first suggestion was to call it 'Four Corners virus', because that is where first case was found; but that would have been bad for tourism and objections were raised. So, it was decided to call it 'Sin Nombre' which is Spanish for 'no name'. This kept everybody happy. However, the question of where this previously unseen virus came from remained. It was quickly established that it was excreted persistently in urine, faeces and saliva of deer mice *(Peromyscus maniculatus)*. In the previous year of the El Niño – La Niña cycle, the deer mice had plenty to eat because the weather conditions had produced lots of grain and berries. Their populations expanded and they moved to new territories. They moved to areas where they had never been before, including the cave where the first identified case was contracted. In total, approximately 50 cases of this new disease were diagnosed in that year and, when records of people who had died from unknown respiratory causes over the same period were examined, it was found there also. From that starting point, the numbers of viruses identified have increased and there are now over 30 different hantaviruses found throughout the New World, they all have a rodent host, the rodents are never affected by it, but they excrete it persistently in urine and faeces.

The UK now has a policy that cats and dogs can be taken backwards and forwards between Britain and continental Europe without quarantine, provided they have been given a rabies vaccine and they are micro-chipped. Before this new legislation, animals had to be quarantined, primarily to prevent the import of rabies into the UK. Britain had not had an indigenous case of rabies since 1922. Being an island is of great advantage in this regard. But the committee that looked at this legislation then realised that there was a problem associated with the greater movement of pets in that there are some ticks and tapeworms that are only found on the continent and not found in Britain. One of these is *Echinococcosis multilocularis*, which causes hydatids disease. Hydatids disease results in multiple cysts, is surgically impossible to get rid of and is uniformly fatal. Hydatids disease is now present on the Atlantic coast of France so all dogs coming into the UK from France are now given Praziquantel so they defecate out the eggs before reaching the UK in order to keep out *E. multilocularis*. Collars that will kill ticks are also required on cats and dogs so *Rhipicephalus sanguineus,* which carries a number of diseases, is not brought into the UK.

In the UK, we now have our own indigenous rabies, European Bat Lyssavirus, with three cases of infection in people. The first case was two people on the south coast of England who found a sick bat and were bitten by it. The second was a bat handler in Scotland who was bitten and developed rabies but nobody recognised it, because he had not been out of the country and it was not considered as part of the differential diagnosis. It does appear, however, that the current rabies vaccine will prevent it.

5.4 New zoonoses emerging in the UK

Vorou *et al.* (2007) reviewed the pathogens that have emerged in Europe from 2000 to 2006 (Figure 5-2) and linked them to social, ecological and technological risk factors. They identified tick-borne encephalitis, *Borellia* spp. (which cause Lyme disease), *Anaplasma* spp., Congo-Crimean Haemorrhagic fever, *Bartonella* spp., *Francisella tularensis,* hantaviruses, Toscana virus and West Nile virus as the main zoonoses or pathogens of concern.

FIGURE 5-2
Emerging Pathogens: Europe 2000–2006 (after Vorou *et al.* 2007)

	SOCIAL	ECOLOGICAL	TECHNOLOGY	AGENT
Tick borne pathogens (tick borne encephalitis, *Borellia* spp., *Anaplasma* spp., Congo-Crimean Haemorrhagic fever)	Leisure activities	Climate or vectors	Increased awareness, better diagnostics	–
***Bartonella* spp.**	Poverty Immunosuppression Pets and lice	Extended spectrum of reservoir host	Advanced diagnostics	–
Francisella tularensis	Political crisis, war, hunting, farming, bioterrorism	War, floods, climate change. Role of hares and cats. Natural water.	Advanced diagnostics	–
Congo-Crimean Haemorrhagic fever	Social and political change	Tick abundance, livstock management, climate		–
Hantaviruses	Leisure activities War	Climate on bank vole populations	Advanced diagnostics	Viral evolution
Toscana virus	Travel	Climate change	Advanced diagnostics	
West Nile	International travel Bird migrations	Climate Horses, birds	Advanced diagnostics	Viral evolution

One reason more of these pathogens are being observed could well be increased awareness and better diagnostics, as the agent does not seem to have changed in many cases. Social factors, such as increased leisure activities and different types of leisure activities, poverty, immunosuppression, pets and travel do play a role however. Ecological factors are also important with climate change or ecosystem change being identified as risk factors for the spread of most of the emerging zoonoses or pathogens.

Most of those zoonoses and pathogens identified by Vorou *et al.* (2007) are not yet found in the UK but are likely to be found here in the near future. The main new zoonoses of concern of emerging in the UK are West Nile fever, Toscana virus, tick-borne encephalitis, *Echinococcus multilocularis* (discussed earlier), Congo-Crimean Haemorrhagic fever, *Francisella tularensis* and *Bartonella* spp.

West Nile fever has emerged in the US, and is now present from Canada down to South America, probably having been carried by birds. So far, it appears that the UK is not affected. Although some claim that West Nile fever is present in the UK already, it is still controversial because the diagnostic test used is disputed. We do, however, have the vectors capable of transmitting the virus here in the UK.

The Toscana virus is a sand fly transmitted virus that has been found in France, Italy and Spain and, should climate conditions become favourable, then it may be brought to the UK. Similarly, tick-borne encephalitis, which is caused by a virus that is found in small rodents or occasionally in larger animals and is transmitted by ticks, will possibly become more common in the UK with climate change. The range of tick-borne encephalitis has already extended as far as the Atlantic coast of France. There are also several *Bartonella* species that could potentially emerge in the UK.

There are probably two hantaviruses in Britain, the Seoul virus in rats and Puumala virus in bank voles. There is little evidence for human infections however. The only evidence is serological; antibodies have been found in people, but nobody has been found with the disease yet.

Fortunately for the UK, the European form of *Francisella tularensis* is less pathogenic than the American form. With the American form the inhalation of just one bacterium is sufficient for infection, 100 or more are required of the European one.

The risks from zoonoses in the UK are, therefore, relatively low currently when compared with other countries. However, climate change and ecosystem change are likely to increase the number and extent of zoonoses that are found in the UK. Clearly, this requires us to be increasingly vigilant, but we should not focus solely on the new and emerging zoonoses and neglect the zoonoses that are already with us and may become more prevalent with climate and ecosystem change.

6

Mycobacterium avium subspecies *paratuberculosis:* diverse opportunities for environmental cycling and human exposure

ROGER PICKUP, LANCASTER UNIVERSITY
GLENN RHODES, CENTRE FOR ECOLOGY AND HYDROLOGY
JOHN HERMON-TAYLOR, KING'S COLLEGE LONDON

6.1 Introduction

Studying pathogens in the environment is problematic for a number of reasons. All environmental microbiological studies are compromised by a number of constraints centring on: sampling and access to representative environmental samples, sample heterogeneity (i.e. is one sample comparable to another from the same area?) and culturability (Pickup 1995). Culturability is always a key issue. For example, hospital-based tests which often underpin successful microbiological diagnoses have limitations when applied to describing pathogens in environmental samples. Culturability is one of the most difficult problems faced because, even if an organism can be cultured in the lab, once it passes through the environment it will not necessarily be possible to culture it again (Rozak and Colwell 1987). The problem of culturability is prevalent in microbiology. If a plate method is used for culturing on a general medium, between 0.1% and 10% of the organisms present are likely to be present as culture. In water samples, it is more likely to be at the lower end of this range (Jones et al. 1979). To put this in perspective, only 1,000 organisms out of a million organisms that are present in lake water are likely to be present as culture, leaving a huge area of undescribed biodiversity. Some pathogens, when they are present in a sample, can become non-culturable but viable (NCBV). *Vibrio cholerae* is a classic example of this (Rozak and Colwell 1987). It is the causative agent of cholera and has the ability to become NCBV in the environment whereby it cannot be detected by plate methods if present in a sample yet those exposed to it may contract the disease. Apart from the NCBV issue, the discrepancy between culturability and total count of bacteria culturing is a product of the selectivity of solid culture media, usually because the nutrient levels are too high causing oxidative stress, but also because some bacteria just do not like surfaces. In short, in many instances, the environment in which bacteria live cannot be recreated on the plate. Culture methods are not therefore necessarily the best techniques to investigate micro-organisms, but they do underpin most studies and provide a reference standard for new techniques (Pickup 1995). If pathogens can be identified either by culture or molecular methods, then identifying their source is very important (Meays et al. 2004; Foley et al. 2009). Source tracking is becoming increasingly important in managing water quality, often focussing on faecal indicator bacteria it allows source to be identified and remedial actions taken (Field and Samadpour 2007) .

6.2 Cycling of Mycobacterium avium subspecies paratuberculosis in the environment and links to Crohn's disease

Other papers in this volume (Chapter 4 and Chapter 5) have highlighted the role of the environment and ecosystems as transport mechanisms for disease. *Mycobacterium avium* subspecies *paratuberculosis* (MAP) can be used to illustrate this further in a UK context. Pickup *et al.* (2005) examined the distribution of MAP in the River Taff catchment in South Wales and looked at its potential relationship to a clustering of Crohn's disease cases in Cardiff. MAP causes Johne's disease in animals, which is a debilitating disease characterised by damage to the intestines that results in diarrhoea, weight loss, loss of condition and infertility (Chiodini *et al.* 1984). Infected animals excrete MAP into the environment in extremely large numbers. Slurry spreading and other farm practices can further spread MAP. The organism itself has a broad pathogenicity; domestic and wild ruminants, deer, alpaca, horses, pigs, dogs, rabbits and predators, chickens and carrion birds are among its susceptible hosts. It is also recognised as a pathogen in a number of primates, but it is not widely recognised as a pathogen in humans.

MAP is implicated as a cause of Crohn's disease and, more recently, Irritable Bowel Syndrome (IBS) in humans, although these links are controversial (Scanu *et al.* 2007). There is no current consensus on the link between MAP and Crohn's disease, although work is progressing continuously on establishing whether there is a link or not (Abubakar *et al.* 2008). MAP has been reported in between 0–93% of all human tissue from people with Crohn's disease. It is a difficult organism to detect, which accounts for the lower reporting in this range of figures. The fact that Johne's disease is increasing in the UK is not disputed. Crohn's disease is rising Europe-wide too, particularly in children. Within children, there has been a seven-fold increase in incidence over approximately the last ten years (Hildebrand *et al.* 2003). A DEFRA study, concluded, however, that there is no proven link between MAP and Crohn's disease (Abubakar *et al.* 2007). From that study, there were two explanations for the lack of a causal link. Firstly, that there is actually no causal link and, secondly that there is a causal link but the study design was unable to detect it. The reasons they put forward for the second explanation were the possible ubiquity of the organism in the environment, which was not in the model used but has been shown by Pickup and co-workers (2005, 2006), and exposure routes that were not taken into account, for example, exposure from milk and dairy products and water (river, potable and aerosols: Ibrahim Abubakar, powerpoint presentation Health Protection Agency 2006). Since then the close association between MAP and Crohn's disease has been recognised (Abubakar *et al.* 2008), but it has not been recognised as a causal agent.

6.3 UK case studies

Research has focused attention on exposure routes through milk and dairy products and water (Millar *et al.* 1996, Pickup *et al.* 2005). Millar *et al.* (1996), using a molecular method, found that approximately 12% of all retail pasteurised milk contained MAP. In the most recent studies, MAP was reported to be present in 9.8% of samples in the Republic of Ireland using polymerase chain reaction (PCR) detection (O'Reilly *et al.* 2004). In the USA, 2.8% of samples have been found to contain culturable MAP (Ellingson *et al.* 2005). Similarly, in the Czech Republic (Ayele *et al.* 2005) and in Argentina (Cirone *et al.* 2007) culturable MAP has been identified in retail milk samples. It appears, therefore, MAP appearing in milk is a worldwide problem.

Pickup *et al.* (2005) investigated the waterborne transmission of MAP from animals to humans in South Wales. The driver for the study was the assumption that MAP is implicated Crohn's disease and that the environmental source of MAP is known to be from diseased animals. It was also assumed that there is a certain amount of cycling in the environment, which could be tracked using molecular methods comprising PCR based assay for detection of insertion sequence 900 *(IS900)* as a marker sequence. It was thought that if Crohn's disease does involve MAP then it must have an infection route, which may be an environmental one. It is known that bacterial pathogens are extremely good at surviving in the environment, including ones that are not commonly associated with the environment, as is the case for MAP (Pickup *et al.* 2005).

MAP is difficult to culture compared with other bacteria. With *E-coli,* for instance, visible colonies form in culture within about twelve hours. With MAP, even using a good lab strain, it may take about six weeks to get colonies, and even longer from an environmental sample (for example, Pickup *et al.* 2006 found that it took 11 months). In parallel laboratory studies it was shown that MAP in sterile lake water was culturable for 632 days, which is a long period of time for micro-organisms, but it was also detectable by molecular techniques for more than 841 days. This demonstrates that it has a significant ability to survive in the environment (Pickup *et al.* 2006).

The hypothesis for the study (Pickup *et al.* 2005; Pickup *et al.* 2006) was that MAP was present in the Rivers Taff and Tywi, and Lake District catchments; it is associated with sediments and is therefore also suspended in the water column. It was also thought that it might be contained within biofilm communities, as with some other pathogens (e.g *Legionella pneumonia*). It was also hypothesised that MAP is present in the holding reservoirs where domestic water supplies are abstracted from the River Tywi (the River Taff is not an abstraction river) and a profile of MAP could be found in sedimentary cores. Its presence in sedimentary cores could give a historical record of co-emergence with industrialisation and intensive farming. The River Taff was included in the study as it is a spate river with Cardiff, a highly populated area, at the lower end of the catchment. Land use includes hill pastures grazed by livestock and MAP is endemic in the herds within the catchment. There is also a published distribution of Crohn's disease patients, with an identified association to the river Taff (Mayberry 1989; Mayberry and Hitchens 1978; Mayberry et al. 1979).

The main river above Cardiff was sampled twice-weekly from November 2001 to November 2002 and additional samples were taken in the upper sub-catchments. Bottom sediment samples and cores were taken from reservoirs within the catchment. To increase confidence in the results, the study used more controls in the PCR method than would typically be used and, once identified by the size of the DNA sequence, it was further confirmed by sequencing the whole piece of DNA. If shown to be within a certain percentage of similarity to the base MAP strain then MAP was considered to be present. A sample found to be positive for MAP, therefore, is extremely likely to be a true positive. Using the PCR method however, a negative result it does not necessarily mean that a sample is negative for MAP as the presence of other substances, for instance, humic acid, can inhibit these molecular methods. There are also issues of the patchiness of sampling and the problems with sampling the environment mentioned above. The study results, therefore, show the minimum number of samples that were positive for MAP and may be underestimating the true extent of MAP within the catchment (Pickup et al. 2005).

Figure 6-1 shows a time series of flow and water level in the River Taff and the occurrence of positive and negative samples for MAP taken within the urban section of the river in Cardiff. During the period November 2001 to November 2002, 32% of the samples were positive for MAP and there was a significant association of positive samples with rainfall, although their presence could not be predicted from rainfall, river flow or river level data (Pickup et al. 2005).

The sediment cores taken in the reservoirs retain their stratification so that, using assumptions about the sediment deposition rate, a time series can be generated showing when the material in different parts of the core was deposited. Of the four reservoirs sampled, two were negative and two were positive for MAP in the sediment cores below the surface. The analysis showed that the organism was deposited over a 20–40 year period prior to sampling, demonstrating that it is present historically within the catchment (Pickup et al. 2005).

FIGURE 6-1
Presence of IS900 in the River Taff from November 2001 to November 2002.
Black diamonds indicate samples positive for MAP, grey diamonds indicate samples negative
for MAP (Pickup *et al.* 2005)

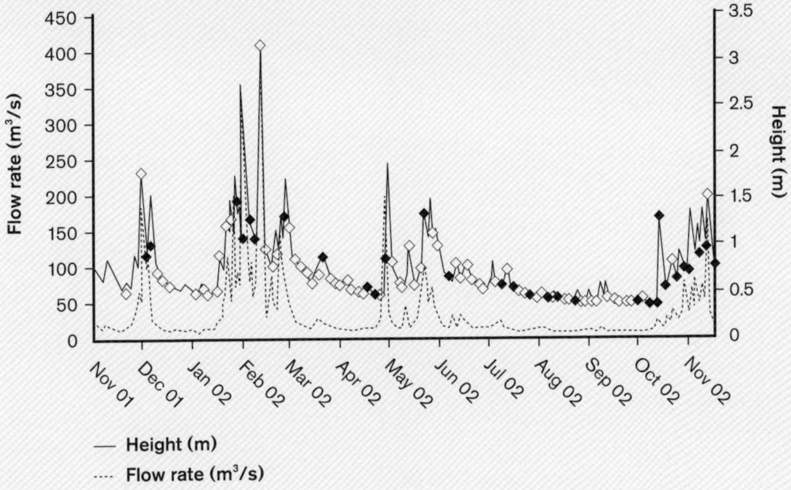

Previous studies of the distribution of Crohn's disease patients have shown that there is an
association with the river, there being significantly higher numbers of cases following the
valley of the River Taff (Mayberry and Hitchens 1978). There is, however, one area on the
prevailing windward side which is within a valley open to the prevailing south-westerly winds
that does not follow this pattern and has a lower incidence of cases than surrounding areas.
Pickup *et al.* (2005) hypothesised, given their results showing the extent of MAP contamination
within the river, that the higher density of Crohn's disease cases following the river valley may
be due to aerosols from the river transporting MAP into the populated areas, increasing the
incidence above the background to more significant levels. The combination of topography
and prevailing meteorological conditions influencing the movement of aerosols from the river
then explains the occurrence of the low incidence area directly opposite a valley open to the
prevailing winds. Further work is in progress to test this hypothesis.

FIGURE 6-2
Flow rate, rainfall and MAP samples for the River Tywi (Pickup *et al.* 2006). Black diamonds indicate samples positive for MAP, grey diamonds indicate samples negative for MAP.

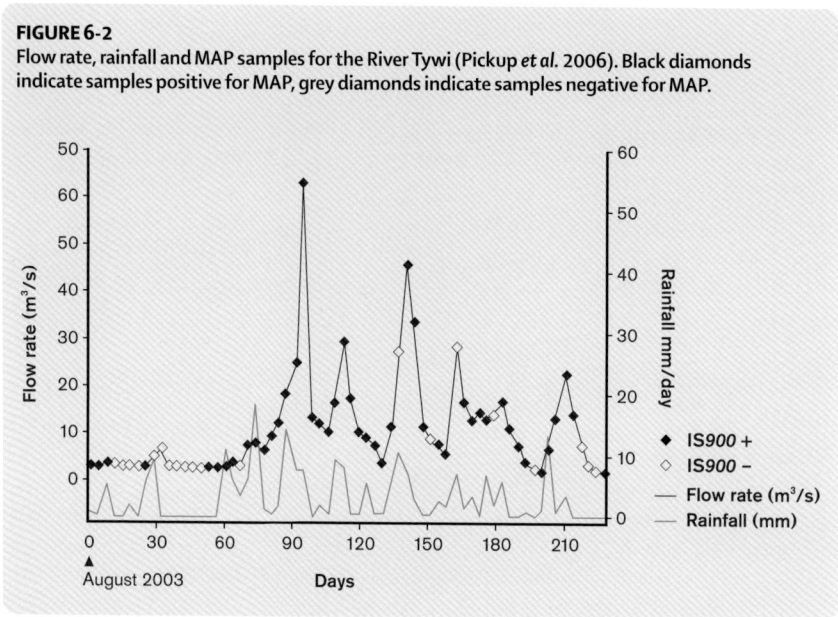

Pickup *et al.* (2006) also investigated MAP within the River Tywi catchment in South Wales. The River Tywi catchment is a larger catchment adjacent to the River Taff. As with the River Taff, it is a spate river, but an important difference between the two catchments is that the River Tywi provides water for abstraction to public supply, which is not the case in the River Taff. Hill pastures grazed by livestock dominate the upper catchment and MAP is endemic in this area. The river was sampled just upstream of the abstraction point for the water treatment works twice weekly for a period of seven months from August 2002 to April 2003, with other sampling taking place in the upper sub-catchments, and cores and bottom sediment samples taken from reservoirs. The water treatment system was also sampled.

In the higher part of the catchment where there is very little sediment and the river is fast flowing and small, no samples were found to contain MAP, but the lower part of the catchment, which is more associated with pasture, had a high rate of positive samples. Figure 6-2 shows the samples found positive and negative for MAP against the river flow rates and rainfall from August 2003 to April 2004 at Nantgaredig Bridge near Carmarthen (Wales). From the samples taken at Nantgaredig Bridge 69% were positive for MAP, compared with 32% for the River Taff study (Pickup *et al.* 2006).

There is, therefore, a significant difference between the rural Tywi catchment and the more urban area sampled in the Taff catchment. In the case of the Tywi, there is a significant association between MAP and the river hydrography. River flow rates were significantly associated with the presence of MAP. For a flow above 3.4 m³/s the presence of MAP in the river could be predicted. Pickup *et al.* (2006) were also able to show that the presence of MAP could be associated with rainfall up to seven days before the positive sample. There was also clustering of positive samples giving prolonged pulses of MAP for up to eight weeks in the river followed by a gap and then further pulses. These pulses were clearly influenced by rainfall.

The water abstraction system from the River Tywi and the Felindre water treatment works, which is about 21 kilometres away and receives the water from the Tywi abstraction point via a pipeline, were also sampled for MAP. The abstraction point on the River Tywi is about 200 metres below the Nantgaredig Bridge, where significant numbers of MAP positive water samples had already been found. Sludge samples and sediment from the river bank opposite the abstraction point were found to be MAP positive. In the treatment works itself, the holding reservoir was found to be MAP negative, although sampling difficulties may have been the cause of this. Within the Counter Current Dissolved Air Flotation and Filtration Plant in the water treatment works, MAP was significantly associated with the sediment. The sediment that comes out of the water purification is deposited in sludge lagoons to dry, which was also found to contain MAP. This is significant for the distribution model for MAP because this sludge is returned to the land (Pickup *et al.* 2006).

Sampling was also undertaken in the homes of some Crohn's patients and non-Crohn's patients. Sampling of potable water had already been shown to be negative for MAP, but for this study areas in the home where there is likely to be some residual sediment from the water treatment process present were sampled (e.g. cold water tanks and toilet cisterns). One out of 70 samples was positive, which is not significant, but a larger study might potentially show that MAP gets through the water treatment system. This would not be particularly surprising because it is a very robust organism, but this hypothesis needs further investigation (Pickup *et al.* 2006).

Sampling in the Lake District also found that all the lakes in the northern part of the Lake District contain MAP (Pickup *et al.* 2006). Focusing on the Windermere catchment, the two high tarns, Easedale Tarn and Codale Tarn, were found to be MAP positive, as was the quaternary treated sewage effluent from Ambleside treatment works, which discharges effluent in to Windermere itself. MAP was also found in the sediment cores of Windermere and Esthwaite Water, with its depth suggesting that is has been deposited continuously since 1950, or possibly before that date (Pickup *et al.* 2006).

FIGURE 6-3
Conceptual model of MAP pathways through the environment (Pickup *et al.* 2006).

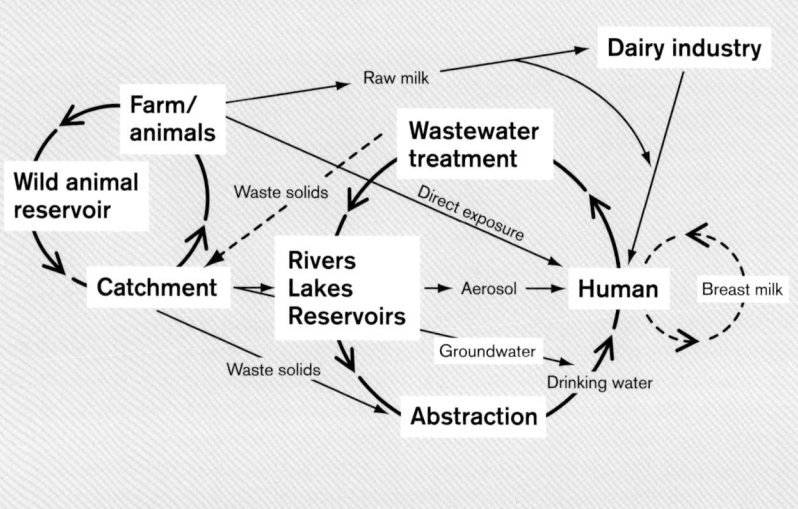

6.4 Conclusions

Overall, this work has demonstrated that MAP is present in three independent and large catchments (Taff, Tywi and Windermere) (Pickup *et al.* 2005, Pickup *et al.* 2006). The geography and the rainfall influence its presence. It has a possible exit route via aerosols. It has a high survival potential (more than three years in the laboratory) and sediment cores can show a historical deposition record. It is also clear that water treatment can reduce numbers of MAP, but there is a possibility that could be transferred to the water distribution system as it has been found in water tanks supplied with potable/treated water. There is a possible association with sediment rather than in the river water itself, as it is not particularly abundant in stony areas and is more prevalent in lower reaches with areas of sediment deposition. MAP was also found within biofilms, but it is unknown whether it is within the amobea or just caught in the biofilm. However, laboratory work (Mura *et al.* 2006) has demonstrated a very long association between MAP and *Acanthamoeba polyphage*. Not only does it survive for three years within *Acanthamoeba polyphage,* so as it divides the MAP itself is transferred, but micro array analysis reveals that the genes assumed to be involved in the pathogenicity of MAP are switched on to a very high level.

These conclusions lead to a conceptual model for the flow of MAP through the catchment and on to human exposure (see Figure 6-3; Pickup *et al.* 2006). There is an animal reservoir in wild animals and farm animals, which contributes MAP to the land surface of the catchment and this is carried through to lakes and rivers, leading to human exposure as an aerosol and, possibly, through drinking water. There are other possible exposure routes to humans through dairy products

An important consideration within the water abstraction and effluent treatment processes is that the waste solids from treatment can be heavily contaminated with MAP and can be returned to the catchment by being spread on farmland. This presents the possibility of a mixture of the animal and human strains of MAP. There is a hypothesised connection in the model presented in Figure 6-3 with drinking water via groundwater but this has not been found yet in practice, possibly because MAP is filtered out in the topsoils. There is also a concern with breast milk as some mothers with Crohn's disease may pass MAP their children (Naser *et al.* 2000). Raw milk from the dairy industry also poses a risk for transmission of MAP to humans (Millar *et al.* 1996). There are, therefore, diverse opportunities for humans to be exposed to MAP (Pickup *et al.* 2006).

Putting this into the context of zoonoses in general, the methods outlined here for following MAP through catchments are just as applicable to other pathogens (e.g. *Campylobacter, E-coli* etc.) and demonstrate the importance of taking a system-wide view of the reservoirs and transport mechanisms for pathogens (Pickup *et al.* 2003). It has also demonstrated that with effort and a lot of sampling these links can be established (Pickup *et al.* 2005, Pickup *et al.* 2006).

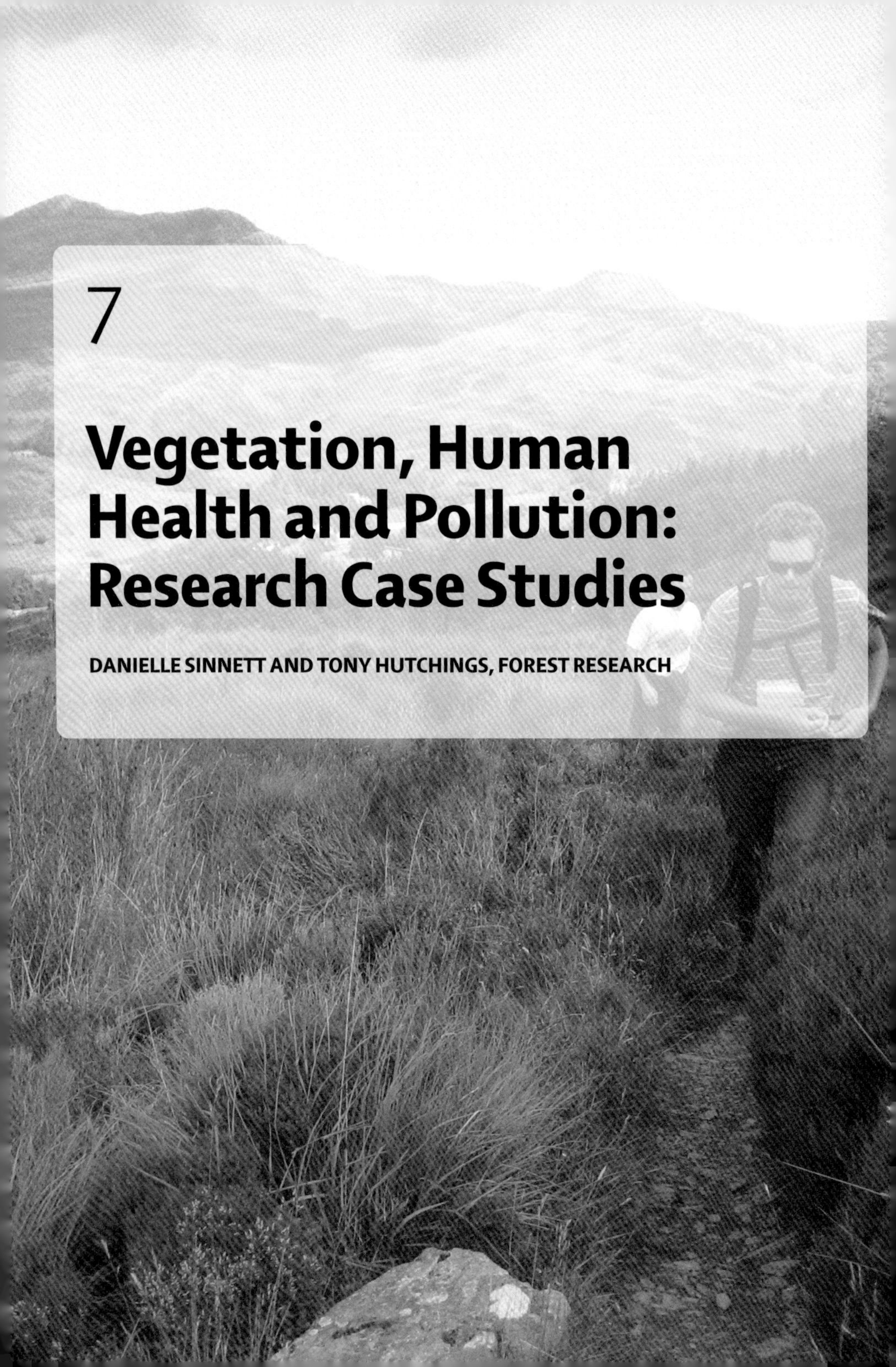

7

Vegetation, Human Health and Pollution: Research Case Studies

DANIELLE SINNETT AND TONY HUTCHINGS, FOREST RESEARCH

7.1 Introduction

Green space creation can bring a substantial range of benefits to a community or region. These can be characterised as social, environmental and economic and may include improvements to the aesthetic, amenity and educational value of an area, an increase in community ownership, as well as improving the health and well-being of the local population. Green space can also provide a semi-natural habitat, protect and link existing habitats and promote biodiversity. These functions may ultimately result in an increase in land value, property prices and inward investment.

Such impacts are particularly true of contaminated and brownfield sites, which are often in areas that have seen large industrialisation in the past, and often have little green space provision. In addition, many of these areas have suffered economic decline in recent decades and have not had the inward investment required to clean up and return derelict sites back to beneficial use. Also, the rate of dereliction in some areas continues to exceed the rate of regeneration. The National Land Use Database of Previously Developed and Buildings (NLUD-PDL) shows that, although there has been a reduction in the area occupied by derelict and/or vacant land and buildings in England between 2001 to 2006 (from 41000 ha to 34850 ha), there is a significant amount of regional variation, with London having less than 1000 ha and the North West having around 7000 ha in 2006 (English Partnerships 2007a). In addition, this database shows that in 2006 51 % of all previously developed land is in urban areas, primarily within regions such as Greater Manchester, Merseyside, Teesside, and Tyne and Wear (English Partnerships 2007b). The creation of new green space offers a relatively cost-effective option to restore these sites to a beneficial end use that will improve the aesthetic appearance of the area and help drive future social and economic regeneration of surrounding areas.

There is a large programme of land regeneration projects currently underway across the UK. These involve the reclamation or remediation of a large range of sites, from under-managed green space to mineral extraction sites, landfills and other waste disposal sites, to contaminated sites. A large number of partners and stakeholders are often involved in the process including the Forestry Commission, Groundwork, Regional Development Agencies, Local Authorities, community groups and NGOs. Whilst green space provision is often seen as a low-cost option for many sites, the recognised benefits of this land use are illustrated in the total amount of funding currently being made available for regeneration projects. The Forestry Commission's land regeneration projects alone, for instance, are costing in excess of £100 million.

Pollution may impact significantly on the health of both human and ecological receptors. Figure 7-1 shows the variety of pollutant pathways that may exist as a result of past or present industrial activity. Any regeneration project on contaminated land must be sensitive to both the contaminants present at a site and also the pathways that might exist or be created by the land regeneration process. The land regeneration process must aim to break these pathways in order to reduce to acceptable levels the risks to people visiting the sites, ecological receptors that may exist there and ground and surface water quality. In addition, many degraded sites will not support sustainable vegetation establishment without some form of remedial action. This may be as basic as cultivation to remove soil compaction, but where contamination is present it can also mean removal or treatment of soil material.

This paper concentrates on three examples of pollutant pathways through air, soil and water, and how research conducted by Forest Research has demonstrated that, through green space creation, it is possible to reduce the impact of these pathways on both human and ecological receptors.

FIGURE 7-1
Examples of pollutant pathways resulting from past and present urban activities and controlling factors for pollutant transport.

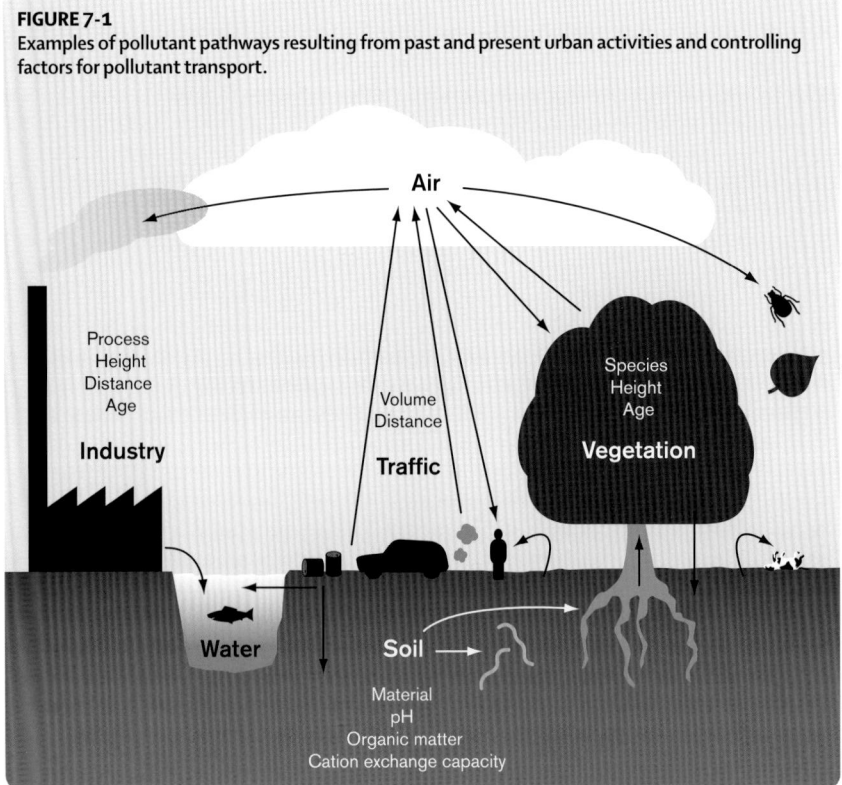

7.2 Reducing the risks of water pollution in the River Tamar

7.2.1Background

The Devon Great Consols mine in south Devon is one of over one hundred old tin mines within the Tamar Valley. The mining process resulted in large spoil tips being deposited. The spoil has high concentrations of a range of contaminants, particularly arsenic (As) but also cadmium (Cd) and lead (Pb).

These tips are largely unvegetated and a project completed by Forest Research and the University of Reading at Devon Great Consols found that spoil materials are eroding during rainfall events and washing into tributaries of the Tamar River. This is creating up to 25 g/L of suspended and 3500 g/m^2 of bedload sediment in the tributary streams, resulting in As concentrations in the tributaries of up to 1500 µg As/L (Mortimore 2007). The Devon Great Consols spoil heaps contribute more than 15% of the total As in the Tamar River (Mortimore, 2007). This constitutes a significant risk to human health as well as to the aquatic systems as the concentration of As in the River Tamar is often above both the Dutch Indicator Values of 5 µg/L and World Health Organisation standard of 10 µg/L. A study by Farago et al. (1997) found that the urine of people living in former tin mining areas had significantly higher As concentrations than those from non-mining areas.

Part of a study funded by the Sustainable Urban Brownfield Regeneration: Integrated Management (SUBR:IM) consortium aimed to ascertain the impact of vegetating the Devon Great Consols spoil heaps on the erosion processes. The effects that vegetation may have on the erosion processes were examined using a water erosion model, the Revised Universal Soil Loss Equation (RUSLE2), developed by the USEPA (Foster, 2004). The RUSLE2 model has a number of components requiring data on climate (e.g. mean annual erosivity (R), Erodability Index (EI) distribution, 10 year-EI, mean monthly rainfall, mean monthly temperature), soil (e.g. structure, texture, surface hydrologic soil class, rock cover and coarse fragment, inherent organic matter, soil profile permeability), topography (e.g. slope steepness, slope length), vegetation and land use. A more detailed account of this work can be found in De Munck et al. (2008).

The model was populated with data from a spoil characterisation project with the University of Reading (Mortimore 2007) and data from the Meteorological Office. We compared the current scenario of bare spoil with two yields of permanent grassland: 3.9 t/ha as a 'standard' grass yield and 1.95 t/ha to explore the consequences of a sub-optimal cover.

Contaminated land remediation must be sustainable and this is an extremely important consideration when using vegetation as a remediation method, given climate change. Climate change is predicted to result in higher rainfall during winter months with an increase in the intensity of storm events. This is likely to have significant impact on erosion processes. In order to ensure that the use of a grass cover to reduce erosion at the Devon Great Consols site will be sustained in the future, data from the UK Climate Impacts Programme (UKCIP) 2002 scenarios for the 2020s, 2050s and 2080s were used in the RUSLE2 model.

7.2.2 Results

De Munck *et al.* (2008) found that the erosion rates are significantly reduced by grass cover from around 100 t/ha/yr to 1.5 and 10 t/ha/yr under the 3.9 and 1.95 t/ha grass yields respectively (Figure 2a). In addition, the mass of As, Cd and Pb that are eroded under bare spoil is substantially reduced by a grass cover with a yield of 3.9 t/ha (Figure 2b).

FIGURE 7-2
Results of RUSLE2 modelling on the use of grass to reduce a) the erosion rates and b) the mass of metal entering the river system at Devon Great Consols (from De Munck *et al.* 2008)

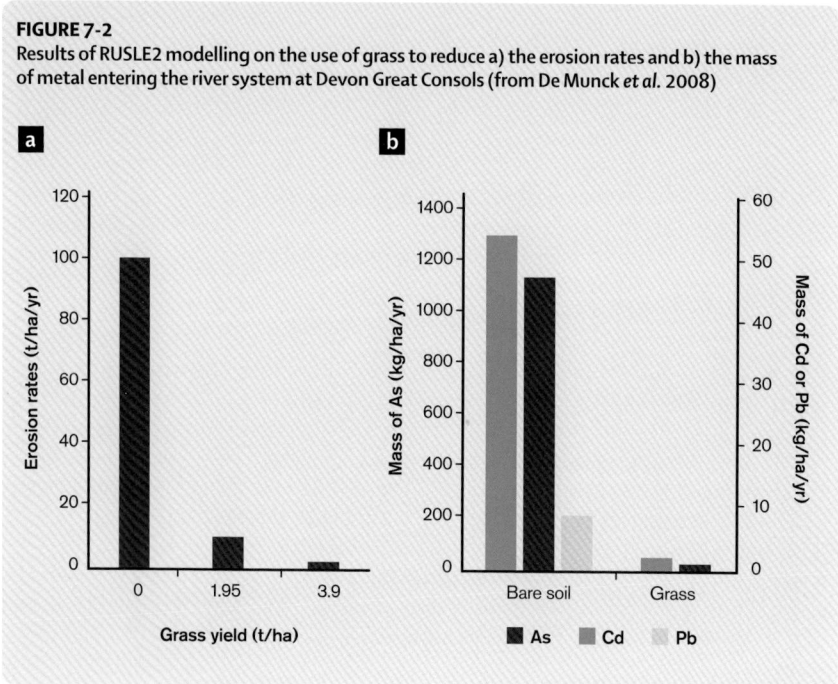

De Munck *et al.* (2008) also found that the erosion rates at Devon Great Consols are predicted to increase under the three UKCIP scenarios (Figure 7-3a). The high emission scenarios are predicted to result in a larger increase in erosion than the low emission scenarios. Under the high emission scenarios erosion rates are predicted to be about 30% greater than the baseline condition by 2080 under unvegetated conditions, compared to 10% greater under the low emission scenarios. By comparison, under either grass cover scenario it is predicted that there will be only a small net increase in the erosion rates under climate change (see Figure 7-3b). Erosion rates were found to be about two orders of magnitude lower for the standard grass yield than for bare spoil.

FIGURE 7-3
Results of the RUSLE2 modelling of a) the impacts of climate change on erosion rates and b) the impact of grass on erosion rates under the high emission scenarios at Devon Great Consols (from De Munck *et al.* 2008)

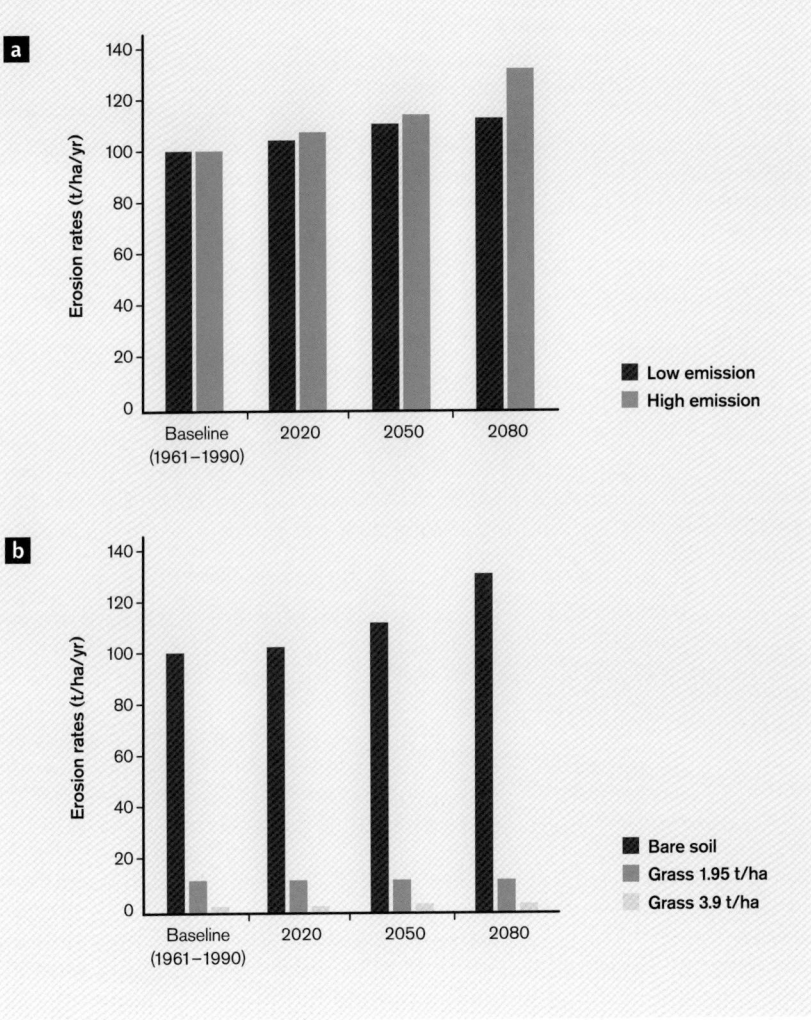

7.3 Remediating contaminated land using soil amendments

7.3.1 Background

Part IIA of the Environmental Protection Act was introduced in England in 2000 (Department of the Environment, Transport and the Regions, 2000) and has subsequently been adopted by Wales and Scotland. This is the legislatory framework for dealing with contaminated land in the UK. It defines contaminated land as that from which there is a significant harm or a significant risk of significant harm to a range of receptors. The receptors include human health, controlled waters, livestock, property and crops, as well as specified ecological receptors including Sites of Special Scientific Interest (SSSI) and Ramsar sites.

A site is defined as being contaminated when a significant source-pathway-receptor linkage is present or is likely to be present. Once deemed to be contaminated a remediation option must be identified that will remove the source of the contamination, break the pathway or remove the receptor. It is often not practical, particularly with ecological receptors, to remove the receptor. For many sites the removal of the contaminant source, for example to landfill or incineration, is often prohibitively expensive for development, particularly to green space.

Another potential remediation option, which can be very cost effective, involves the use of soil amendments to immobilise the contaminants and therefore break the pathway to both human and ecological receptors. Soil amendments can offer a range of benefits to vegetation establishment including their ability to immobilise or degrade both inorganic and organic contaminants, supply plant nutrients, and improve soil structure and water-holding capacity. It is also not energy or resource intensive, can be up to 1% of the cost of landfill, is *in situ* and can be carbon positive and robust. It can also reduce on-site 'waste', the need for topsoil and, ultimately, society's 'waste' burden.

Material from the Devon Great Consols spoil tips and land surrounding the former Avonmouth zinc smelter represent soils with different properties, contaminants and contamination histories. The Devon Great Consols is a mine spoil with no organic matter, a poor structure, a pH of approximately 7 and contaminant concentrations of As >35000 mg/kg, Cd >800 mg/kg and Cu >1600 mg/kg, whilst the Avonmouth soils are silty clays with approximately 6% organic matter, a pH of approximately 6 and metal concentrations of between 20–200 mg/kg for As, 10–200 mg/kg for Cd, 45–220 mg/kg for Cu, 315–16000 mg/kg for Pb and 1000–10000 mg/kg for Zn.

Gadepalle *et al.* (2006) and van Herwijnen *et al.* (2007a, 2007b) mixed these soils with different combinations of different organic and inorganic amendments to test whether the amendment would reduce the mobility of the metal fraction that would be likely to leach and become bioavailable. In addition, plants were grown in the soil following a range of amendment treatments and the metal concentration in the plant tissue measured as another indication of plant availability and toxicity.

7.3.2 Results

It was found by van Herwijnen *et al.* (2007a) that in the Avonmouth soils the leachable Zn concentrations actually increase with addition of sewage sludge and spent mushroom composts compared to the unamended control, whilst green waste compost and LimeX (a commercial product for the regulation of soil acidity) significantly reduced them. However, the plant concentrations suggest green waste compost, spent mushroom compost and LimeX all reduced plant uptake (Figure 7-4 a and b). Whilst this was also true for Cu uptake, the leaching experiment suggested that the mobility of Cu was increased with all amendments compared to the control (Figure 7-4 c and d).

FIGURE 7-4
Results of soil amendment experiments on a) leachable Zn, b) plant Zn, c) leachable Cu and d) plant Cu on Devon Great Consols soils and e) leachable Zn and f) leachable Cu on Avonmouth soils (from van Herwijnen et al. 2007a). GWC = Green waste compost, SC = Composted sewage sludge, SMC = Spent mushroom compost, LX = LimeX70 (sugar refining residue), CC = Coir compost (coconut husk), ▨ metal originates from compost.

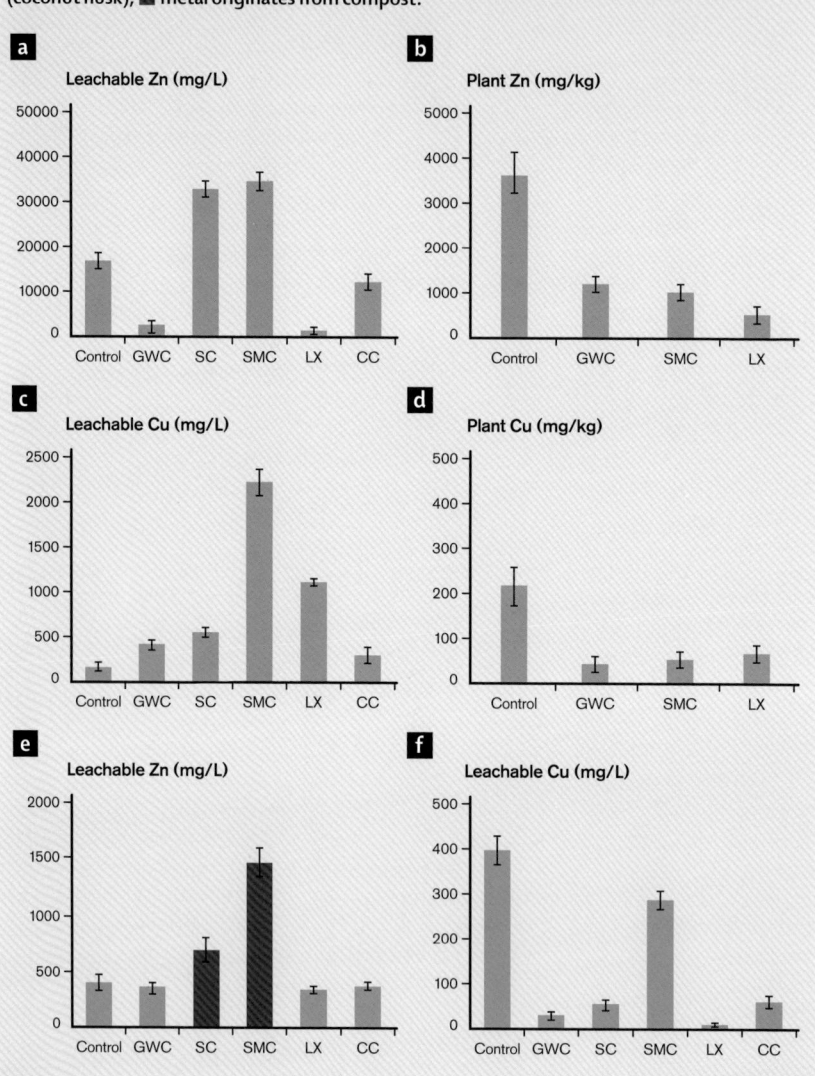

Van Herwijnen *et al.* (2007a) compared this with the leachable Zn and Cu from amended Avonmouth soils to demonstrate the importance of the soil on the effectiveness of the amendment. The Devon Great Consols spoil has a relatively low Zn concentration compared to the Avonmouth soil and as a result the sewage sludge and spent mushroom composts actually significantly increased the total Zn burden. All the amendments reduced the leachable Cu compared to the control. These results showed that it is imperative to use leaching and bioavailability tests in combination prior to using soil amendments in the field.

It is also possible to combine different amendments to increase the potential target immobilisation of contaminants. Gadepalle *et al.* (2006) demonstrated this by using different combinations of amendments to reduce to amount of leachable As from the Devon Great Consols spoil (Figure 7-5). Here a 10% addition of a greenwaste / sewage sludge compost mix did immobilise approximately 10% of the As; but when the compost was combined with a 10% addition of zeolite, immobilisation was decreased by a further 20%. However, when the compost was combined with a 2% addition of iron oxide almost all of the leachable As was removed.

FIGURE 7-5
The effect of different combinations of soil amendments on the leachable As concentrations from the Devon Great Consols soil (from Gadepalle *et al.* 2006) 10c = 10% greenwaste / sewage sludge compost. 10c10z = 10% greenwaste/sewage sludge compost, 10% zeolite. 10c2io = 10% greenwaste/sewage sludge compost, 2% iron oxide (Gadepalle *et al.* 2006)

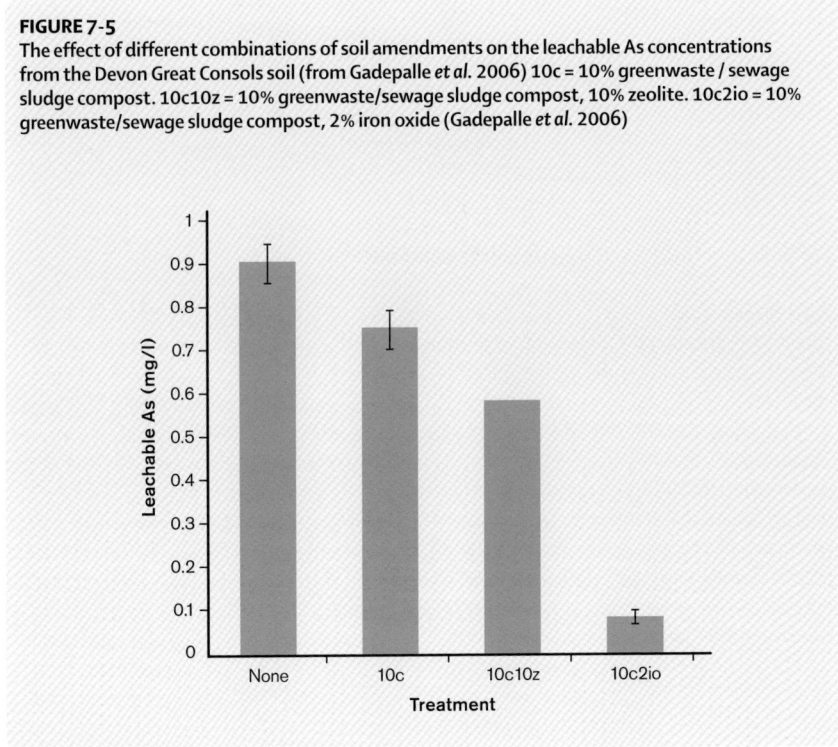

Van Herwijnen *et al.* (2007b) also found that the volume of addition is also extremely important. They found that when green waste compost was used to amend the Avonmouth soil the biomass production of ryegrass increased as the compost addition increased, but that this increase was more dramatic with increasing volumes of sewage sludge compost (Figure 7-6).

FIGURE 7-6
The effect of different proportions of greenwaste and sewage sludge compost on the biomass production of ryegrass (from van Herwijnen *et al.* 2007b). GWC = greenwaste compost. SC = sewage sludge compost

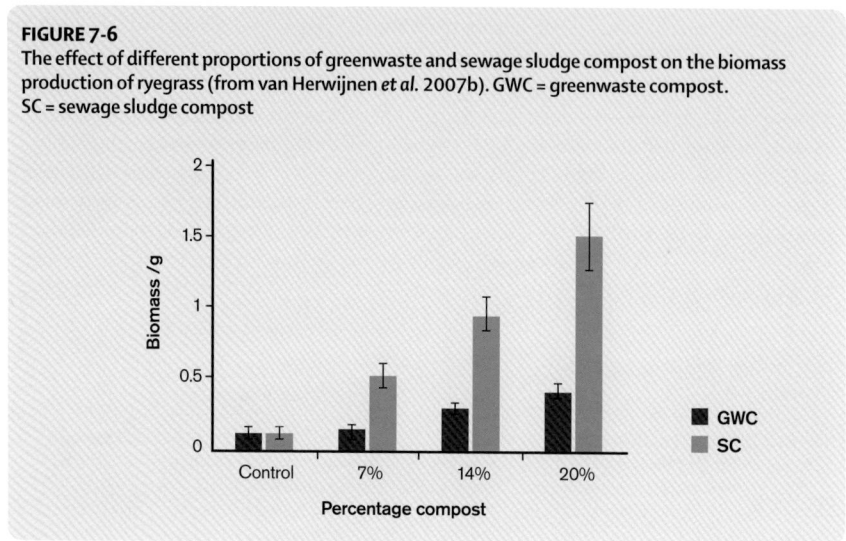

7.4 Reducing the risks of air particulate pollution

7.4.1 Background

Particulate pollution is classified as primary, secondary and coarse. Primary particles are normally less than 2.5 μm in size (often being less than 1.0 μm) and are formed through combustion processes (Air Quality Expert Group (AQEG) 2005). Secondary particles are also normally less than 2.5 μm and are formed in the atmosphere through chemical processes. They include sulphates and nitrates formed through reactions of sulphur dioxide and nitrous oxide (AQEG 2005). Coarse particles are larger than 2.5 μm and come from non-combustion sources including natural sources, such as wind-blown dusts and soils, and man-made sources such as road and tyre dusts and dusts from mining or quarrying (AQEG 2005). The UK air quality standard for particulate matter with a diameter of 10 μm or less (PM_{10}) is 50 μg/m^3 as a 24-hour running mean (not to be exceeded more than 35 times in a calendar year) and the mean annual limit is 40 μg/m^3 (AQEG 2005).

Over the last 15 years PM_{10} concentrations have decreased significantly due to a move away from coal to natural gas in electricity generation, improvements in coal-fired power stations and newer diesel engines capable of meeting tighter emission regulations (AQEG 2005). Despite this, many urban areas within the UK still breach the air quality standards set to be protective of human health.

Many studies have shown that vegetation, particularly trees, can intercept particulate pollution and it remove it from the atmosphere (Freer-Smith *et al.* 1997; Beckett *et al.* 2000; Freer-Smith *et al.* 2004). Forest Research has developed an uptake model to predict the amount of gaseous pollutants that could be taken up by trees (Broadmeadow *et al.* 1998). Recently this model has been modified for determining the interception of PM_{10} by trees. This work has been conducted as part of the Pollutants in the Urban Environment (PUrE) consortium.

For the example presented here, a constant PM_{10} concentration of 29 $\mu g/m^3$ has been assumed for a fictional urban area, where the local authority owned green space has been mapped. Whilst the area is fictional, the parks and air concentrations were based on a combination of real scenarios. In order to estimate the effect of vegetation establishment on the existing green spaces, the percentage cover of trees and the proportions of broadleaf versus conifer trees were altered (Pettit *et al.* 2006).

The input parameters for the model included the area of green space, the leaf area index, deposition velocity, wind speed and canopy height. The model gives outputs of the concentration of PM_{10} in the outflowing air, the mass of PM_{10} deposited to trees and the percentage decrease in PM_{10} air concentration. The model assumes that: PM_{10} concentrations are constant within the turbulent boundary layer (650m); atmospheric conditions are neutral throughout the year; there is no edge effect (i.e. it does not consider that street trees and hedges are likely to be more effective than a woodland block); that trees only exist in local authority owned parks and gardens; that the effects of occult and wet deposition are not significant; there is no resuspension of particles from leaf or stem surfaces; and there is no annual dynamics of leaf area index, which means that the effect of broadleaves is likely to be over-estimated. In addition, PM_{10} concentration and wind speed have been spatially and temporally averaged, the green spaces are assumed to be square and any reduction in PM_{10} concentration in outflowing air is assumed to be uniform across the entire urban area.

7.4.2 Results

Figure 7-7 shows the percentage decrease in PM_{10}, on the left axis, and the mass of PM_{10} removed by the green space under different grass and conifer (C) and broadleaf (B) covers on the right axis. Total grass cover provides little PM_{10} mitigation and, as the proportion of tree cover is increased, so does the amount of particulate matter removed. Similarly, if the percentage of conifer trees is increased compared to broadleaf trees the amount of particulate removal increases. Conifer trees have often been reported to remove more particulate pollution than broadleaves due to their denser foliage (Becket et al. 2000). The difference between broadleaves and conifers will be even larger as broadleaves are not in leaf all year round.

FIGURE 7-7
Modelled percentage decrease in PM10 concentration and mass of PM_{10} removed (kg/ha/yr) using different planting designs (C = conifer cover, B = broadleaf cover)

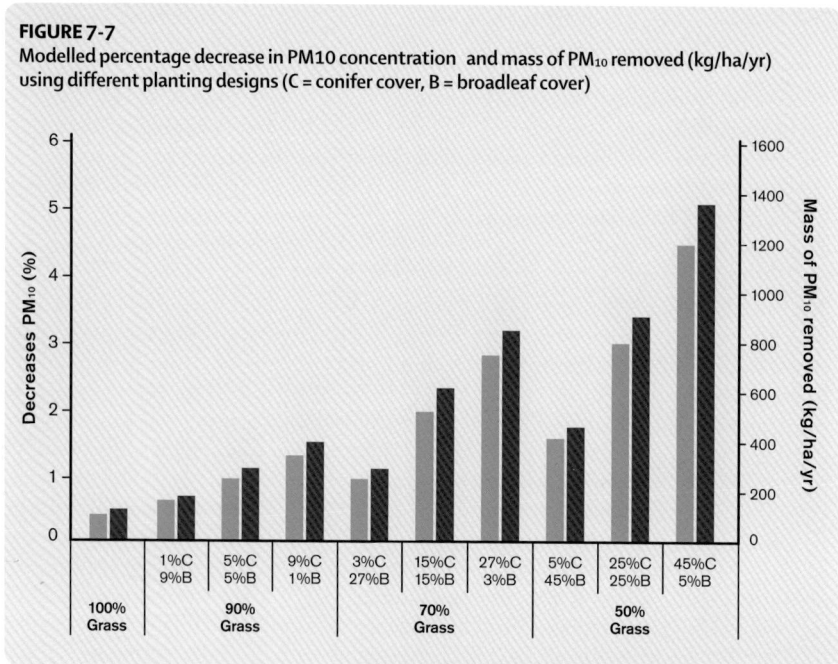

Pettit et al. (2006) also estimated the potential human health effects of PM_{10} pollutants in the urban environment. The human health model used by Pettit et al. (2006) calculated the change in death rate from changes in the PM_{10} concentration above the baseline, the baseline mortality rate, and a co-efficient for the PM_{10}-mortality relationship for a population of just under 500,000. The authors calculated that a reduction in PM_{10} concentration of just over 3% (i.e. as would be the case under 50% tree cover with half broadleaves and half conifers) would result in a reduction of 1.1 deaths per year. In addition, the reduction in PM_{10} is likely to result in a significant reduction in the number of respiratory problems not resulting in death.

7.5 Policy drivers and conclusions

The UK government recognises the importance of green space in communities (ODPM 2003), which has resulted in green space creation frequently being given a higher priority in the planning process. The conversion of contaminated and brownfield land to green space can be particularly beneficial.

The use of green space to stabilise soils, reducing their vulnerability to both water and wind erosion processes, can help to meet a number of environmental quality standards. The ability of trees to reduce air pollution is being recognised increasingly in policy and, as with the use of vegetation for remediation, species selection is vitally important to ensure planting designs are sustainable under future climate scenarios.

England, Scotland and Wales have their own forestry strategies and all recognise the importance of trees, forests and woodland in providing areas for recreation and the ability of these areas to improve the physical health and well-being of the communities around them (DEFRA 2007; Scottish Executive 2006; The National Assembly for Wales 2001). However, all three strategies also specifically mention the use of trees and green space to rehabilitate communities that have suffered from past industrialisation and the impact that greening can have on economic regeneration. If vegetation establishment is to be successful on these types of sites then the toxicological risks must be mitigated in order to protect both human and ecological receptors. The use of soil amendments can be used to achieve successful plant growth and reduce the risks that soil contaminants pose to vegetation. The reduction in mobility of contaminants and their reduced uptake into above ground biomass suggests that amendments will also reduce the risk to both ecological receptors, for example soil invertebrates and primary plant consumers, as well as the people visiting the site.

The use of trees in mitigating air pollution in urban areas is also specifically highlighted as a key objective in both the Scottish and English strategies, and its omission from the Welsh strategy is probably a function of the age of this document compared to the others.

New planting needs to be sympathetic to other issues and objectives within the environment. For example, where the objective is to mitigate the effects of particulate pollution, species selection should also consider the potential pollen and volatile organic compound release of these species. Similarly, the ability of vegetation to tolerate changes in the climate, their ecological value and maintenance requirements should be balanced against the potential benefits they may bring. With these considerations in mind, the establishment of trees and other vegetation in urban areas offers a real opportunity to reduce the risks posed by pollutants to human health.

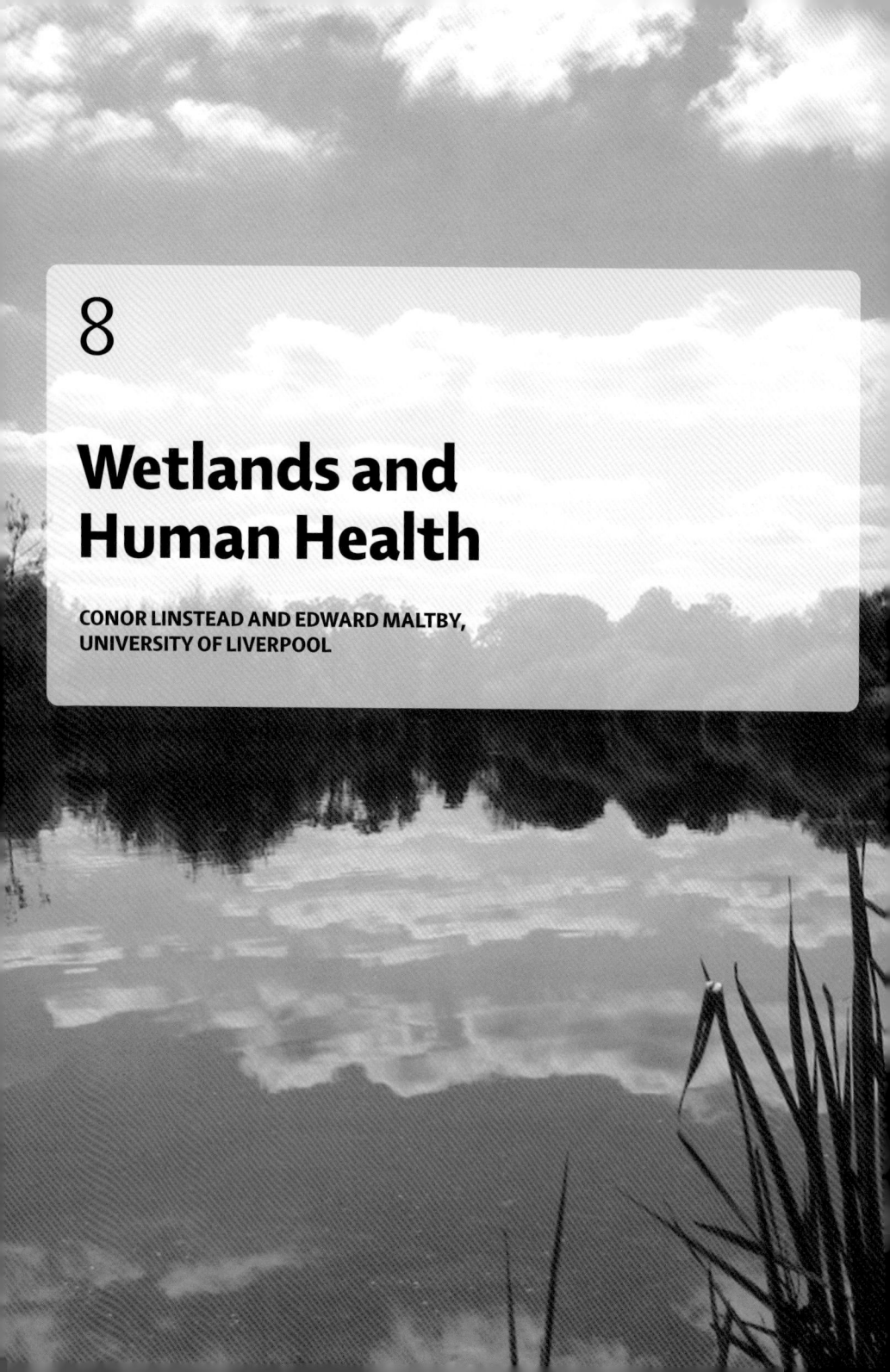

8

Wetlands and Human Health

CONOR LINSTEAD AND EDWARD MALTBY,
UNIVERSITY OF LIVERPOOL

8.1 Introduction

Early human communities were strongly attracted to wetlands along river margins, lake margins and the margins of the sea. Indeed, the 'aquatic ape' theory suggests that the separation of the early hominid ancestors of man from those of the great apes was due to the evolutionary pressures from wading, swimming and diving for food in these types of environments. It is further proposed that the abundance of docosahexaenoic acid in seafood would have allowed the brain to expand in size sufficiently to enable evolution to take man from early *Homo* species to *Homo sapiens*. Although this is not a widely accepted theory, it is certainly the case that early human communities did depend very much on wetlands for resources such as food, materials for shelter and for safety. That perspective of wetlands changed dramatically through subsequent history and wetlands became increasingly viewed as hazardous places and, with the expansion of agriculture, as unproductive wastelands, literally 'wasted-land'. One example of that is the perception of the disease hazard and, in particular, malaria or *mal aria* (bad air) in Italian. Well into the nineteenth century the bad air associated with wetlands was thought to be the cause of the disease and it is worth remembering that malaria was endemic in England until the 1920s with the later recurrences attributed to the introduction or reintroduction of mosquito vectors from the large number of troops returning from overseas after World War I (Chin and Welsby 2004). With the predicted changes in the climate in the future, it is possible that we may see malaria back again in the UK, although modern medicines would prevent it from becoming, as it has in many poorer countries, endemic. This view of wetlands as undesirable, but potentially agriculturally productive areas, has led to continuous loss through drainage, with an accelerated loss beginning with the agricultural policies designed to increase the UK's self-sufficiency with regard to food production introduced in the 1940s until the recent past.

In the last twenty or thirty years, however, the perception of wetlands has changed yet again and the general consensus amongst policy makers, planners and scientists now is that wetlands are undervalued and are good for society because they deliver a wide range of benefits. This change of perception started from a nature conservation standpoint, perhaps beginning with the formation of the Wildfowl and Wetlands Trust in 1946, but is increasingly being linked with the economic valuation of the other benefits of wetlands, such as water quality improvement and flood protection. These benefits are sufficient that there is now a view that wetland restoration, after long periods of destruction, could be a potential means of ameliorating many of the environmental problems we face, and which are likely to increase in magnitude in the face of climate change.

Wetlands were one of the first ecosystem types viewed in the context of the delivery of ecosystem goods and services, and one of the first where economic valuations of those goods and services were attempted (e.g. Costanza *et al.* 1989; Turner *et al.* 1983). Putting this within the structure of the Millennium Ecosystem Assessment (MEA), the delivery of these goods and services can be categorised under the headings of provisioning, regulating, cultural and supporting. Figure 8-1 outlines some of the key ecosystem services delivered by wetlands within this categorisation. The term 'ecosystem service' has become synonymous with both the goods and services from ecosystems, with goods being seen as 'provisioning services' in the context of the MEA and where the term 'ecosystem service' is used here it should be taken to include both goods and services.

The relevance to human health of many of the ecosystem services outlined in Figure 8-1 are clear, particularly in relation to water purification, but many of them only affect human health indirectly. The mechanisms for the effects on human health are through nutrition and food production, provision of water for drinking, cooking and sanitation, materials for shelter, cooking and warmth, medicines, natural hazard protection (flooding, drought, storm damage), reduction of heat stress, reduction of exposure to pollution, physiological and associated mental health benefits from being in natural areas, and opportunities for physical activity through recreation.

Many of these direct and indirect human health services are not particular to wetlands and apply equally to other ecosystem types. The degree to which these services are provided by different ecosystem types does vary, however, and for some services in some contexts wetlands might be a particularly good provider of some ecosystem services. In developing countries, for instance, the key ecosystem services are often the delivery of food and water and these can be strongly associated with wetlands. Rice production, in particular, is associated with wetlands and, compared with other ecosystem types, wetlands are especially valuable for the regulation and purification of drinking and cooking water.

FIGURE 8-1
Wetland Ecosystem Services using the categorisation of the Millennium Ecosystem Assessment (MEA 2005)

SERVICE CATEGORY	SERVICE	COMMENTS AND EXAMPLES
Provisioning	Food	Production of fish, wild game, fruits and grains.
	Fresh water	Storage and retention of water for domestic, industrial and agricultural use.
	Fibre and fuel	Production of logs, fuel wood, peat, fodder.
	Biochemical	Extraction of medicines and other materials from biota.
	Genetic materials	Genes for resistance to plant pathogens, ornamental species and so on.
Regulating	Climate regulation	Source of and sink for greenhouse gases; influence local and regional temperature, precipitation and other climatic processes.
	Water regulation (hydrological flows)	Groundwater recharge/discharge.
	Water purification and waste treatment	Retention, recovery and removal of excess nutrients and other pollutants.
	Erosion regulation	Retention of soils and sediments.
	Natural hazard regulation	Flood control, storm protection.
	Pollination	Habitat for pollinators.
Cultural	Spiritual and inspirational	Source of inspiration; many religions attach spiritual and religious values to aspects of wetland ecosystems.
	Recreational	Opportunities for recreational activities.
	Aesthetic	Many people find beauty or aesthetic value in aspects of wetland ecosystems.
	Educational	Opportunities for formal and informal education and training.
Supporting	Soil formation	Sediment retention and accumulation of organic matter.
	Nutrient cycling	Storage, recycling, processing and acquisition of nutrients.

There are, of course, negatives associated with living in or near wetlands, such as the many disease vectors associated with wetland habitats. However, this can be a complex issue and there is not always a simple relationship between wetland habitats and disease vectors. For example, the conversion of natural wetland areas to rice growing can create more favourable mosquito breeding sites (Huynh and Hai 2002) and lead to a potential increased prevalence of malaria.

In the UK, we have separated ourselves from the immediate reliance on wetlands found in some developing countries for food, fuel, medicines and other ecosystem services that have a direct bearing on health but, nevertheless, there are wetland ecosystem services that have a bearing on health in the UK. Principally these UK-relevant health effects of wetlands relate to the water quality, water flow and erosion regulation functions of wetlands, and the recreation/aesthetic services. Other chapters in this volume have looked in detail at the health benefits from being active in natural or semi-natural environments (see Chapter 2 and Chapter 3) and Chapter 1 touched on the health effects of flooding, which could be mitigated by wetlands, so the following sections will concentrate on how wetlands affect water quality and the implications for human health in a UK context. It is worth noting, however, with regard to wetlands and recreation, that many of the remaining semi-wilderness areas within the UK are wetlands (e.g. upland peat bogs, salt marshes, estuaries) so it could be argued that wetlands are particularly important in the context of allowing people the opportunity to experience semi-wild areas. If there is indeed a dose-response relationship in the physiological and mental health benefits of being in natural areas, with wilder areas giving a greater health response, perhaps wetlands represent the 'intensive care' of this approach to health care.

8.2 Wetlands, water quality and human health

Wetlands are very diverse systems and different types of wetlands function in different ways. For example, some but not all wetland types are peat forming, some are forested, some are not, and they occur in different parts of the landscape, from the uplands to the sea shore. This diversity affects the types of ecosystem services that are provided and the degree to which those services are provided. But some generalisations can be made that, while not true for all wetlands, are frequently the case. The direct effects of wetlands on water quality include reduction of nitrates and phosphates, heavy metals, pesticides, bacteria and viruses. They also provide a buffer between the sources of these contaminants and surface and ground waters that can reduce peaks in concentrations and, hence, acute exposures. There may also be indirect effects on water quality that result from wetlands acting as filters and buffers for pollutants, for example the reduction of nutrients can reduce the risk of blooms of cyanobacteria (Chorus and Bartram 1999), although this happens through a complex series of connections and is highly dependent on the nutrient status of the water bodies concerned.

The processes by which wetlands improve water quality include up-take of nutrients by wetland plants and micro-organisms, promotion of denitrification in anaerobic soil conditions, mineralisation of organic material, long-term storage of organic material, physicochemical adsorption and precipitation in the sediment, lower flow velocities and vegetation structure promoting sediment deposition (with associated pollutants) and diffusion of dissolved nutrients into the sediment (Verhoeven and Mueleman 1999).

Denitrification, in which nitrate is converted in a two stage process firstly to nitrous oxide and then to nitrogen gas, is particularly significant. This is an important process in reducing the potential for eutrophication but, at the same time, it is a potential source of increased global warming through the release of nitrous oxide, which is 310 times more potent as a greenhouse gas than carbon dioxide. This creates an interesting policy dilemma as DEFRA and its agencies promote the protection of surface waters by maximising denitrification control of nitrate-rich runoff, but the full consequences of this in terms of greenhouse gas production are not fully understood.

There has been a considerable amount of research into the value of artificial wetlands i.e. wetlands which have been physically constructed for water quality improvements and which do not necessarily represent natural ecosystems, in reducing the hazards from pesticides, nutrients or other contaminants. In comparison, there is relatively little known about the precise performance of natural wetland ecosystems in the UK. Many of the assumptions that have been made about how natural wetlands work within in the landscape have been inferred from highly artificial systems and systems that often have been monitored for only short periods of time.

FIGURE 8-2
Removal percentages for COD, BOD, nutrients and bacteriological pollution in an infiltration wetland (Verhoeven and Mueleman 1999)

	Loading (t/ha per year)	Removal (%)
COD	18	81
BOD	7	95
Total N	2.8	35
Total P	0.4	26
	Wastewater (n/l (summer))	
F-specific viruses	5.4×10^8	>99.9
E.coli	4.6×10^8	>99.9
MPN Thermotol. bact.	3.9×10^8	>99.9

Nevertheless, these studies of artificial wetlands can tell us something of the potential for natural wetlands to improve water quality. Verhoeven and Mueleman (1999) found a high reduction in chemical oxygen demand (COD), biological oxygen demand (BOD), total nitrogen, total phosphorus and potentially harmful viruses and bacteria in an artificial wetland for wastewater treatment in the Netherlands (see Figure 8-2). The wetland removed approximately one third of nutrients and almost 100% of viruses and bacteria.

Knox et al. (2008) compared changes in water quality provided by a natural, flow-through wetland with a degraded, channelised wetland and found that the natural wetland significantly improved water quality by reducing loads of total suspended sediments, nitrate, and Escherichia coli on average by 77%, 60%, and 68%, respectively, and retained 35–42% of total N, total P, and soluble reactive P (SRP) entering the wetland. Retention of pollutant loads by the channelised wetland was found to be significantly lower than the natural wetland for all pollutants except SRP.

In comparison, a study of a natural riparian floodplain wetland of the River Lambourn showed that 85% of total nitrogen and 70% of total phosphorous were removed under baseflow conditions (Prior and Johnes 2002).

One of the key difficulties in extrapolating from artificial wetlands to natural systems is the period of observation. Many studies have only been carried out for a maximum of three years, and it may be that there is a very effective buffering capacity early on, but after a period of time the ability to retain and process nutrients or other contaminants is reversed and the system starts to become a source of contaminants. In a review of wetland studies, Fisher and Acreman (2004) confirmed that most studies have found that wetlands reduce nitrogen and phosphorus loading, but longer-term studies and those that included frequent monitoring during high flows were more likely to indicate increased loadings.

In the case of the natural environment there is some reluctance to deliberately use wetlands for water treatment or use them as buffers because, by changing the inputs of nutrients in particular, the system ecology will change. If a wetland is valued for its biodiversity, then adding a significant additional load of nutrients is likely to change the ecosystem at a fundamental level. In particular, systems that may be naturally oligotrophic (low in nutrients) but would have the capacity, initially at least, to absorb high levels of nutrients, would change ecologically very quickly through the establishment of species that are more adapted to those high nutrient conditions. Those species adapted to higher nutrient concentrations would tend to out compete those species that are naturally present and adapted to low nutrient conditions. So, the system changes and it becomes less valuable from an ecological standpoint. This implies that we need to look very carefully at the balance between using wetlands to maintain high environmental quality that may be beneficial to human health and retaining values that are important for health in other ways, such as biodiversity.

Wetlands, therefore, have a key role to play in reducing pollution and pathogens in surface and groundwaters, but within the UK almost all water people are exposed to comes through a water treatment system, although bathing waters can also be a significant exposure route.

Drinking water and bathing waters are the two main areas where water quality standards are set by legislation for the protection of human health and that are relevant to wetland ecosystems. Standards set for the protection of human health can be very different to those required for ecosystem protection. In many cases, ecosystems are more sensitive to water quality parameters than humans. For example, safe drinking water limits for nitrate are set at 50 mg/L (set by the Drinking Water Directive), but ecological criteria might set limits at concentrations twenty-five or more times lower (James *et al.* 2005). In other cases, such as bacteriological or viral contamination, ecosystems may be less sensitive than humans and standards are not required for environmental protection.

With respect to drinking water, within the UK water companies are responsible for treating potable water to the required standards as set out in legislation. These regulations are primarily driven by the Drinking Water Directive (98/83/EC). Within the UK, the quality of water treatment is very high: the mean compliance across all water supply zones in 2006 in England and Wales was 99.96% (Drinking Water Inspectorate 2007). Figure 8-3 shows how the percentage of samples failing to meet the standards for nitrate, a key parameter with respect to water quality improvements from wetland ecosystems, has declined over the period 1990–2006.

FIGURE 8-3
Percentage of samples failing to meet the standards for nitrate 1990–2006 (Drinking Water Inspectorate 2007)

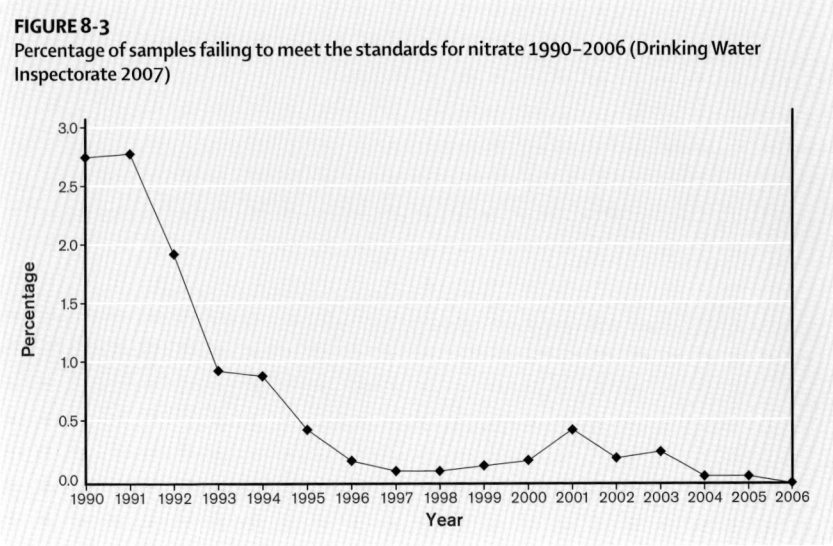

Another key water quality parameter associated with wetlands is Dissolved Organic Carbon (DOC). There has been an increase in the levels of DOC in water from upland peat bogs over the last twenty years. DOC is of concern because it increases the risk of biological contamination of the drinking water supply, because it can form trihalomethanes in the water treatment process, and because it colours the water. Trihalomethanes are toxic and potentially carcinogenic. The reasons for the increased DOC levels are still unclear and may be associated with changes in acidification, altered hydrology and land use and increased temperatures. It is a process that has been recorded not only in the UK but elsewhere in higher latitude regions in the world where peat occurs, suggesting that we are seeing some sort of general environmental change. In northern England in particular, there has been a concern that the effects of drainage ditches or 'gripping' that took place over the last 50 years has been a factor responsible for the dramatic increase in DOC and the removal of DOC has become a high priority for the water utilities in northern England. Although DOC can be removed from the water this intervention is costly and highlights the importance of the ecosystem services provided by wetlands and the potential costs to society of replacing those services when they are lost through ecosystem degradation.

In addition to drinking water, the other key exposure route for people to water in ecosystems is through recreation. Exposure to water through recreation tends not to be long term exposure and the standards for bathing waters put more emphasis on parameters that are important in acute exposures, physical hazards and aesthetics. Bathing water standards in the Bathing Water Directive (76/160/EEC) include standards for ten parameters: total coliforms, faecal coliforms, salmonella, enteroviruses, pH, colour, mineral oils, surface active substances (detergents), phenols and transparency (DEFRA 2009). As discussed above, there is a strong body of evidence that wetlands may be very useful in reducing these key contaminants. The case has certainly been made for artificial wetlands, although there is comparatively little evidence for natural wetlands. The Directive requires that EU Member States identify popular bathing areas and monitor water quality throughout the bathing season (considered in England to be mid May to the end of September). There are 414 sites defined as bathing waters in England, 81 in Wales, 80 in Scotland and 24 in Northern Ireland (DEFRA, 2009). Most of these sites (587) are coastal waters with only 12 being inland freshwater sites, and therefore likely to be significantly influenced by wetlands.

8.3 Conclusions

The main exposure route for people in the UK to pollutants and pathogens in water that can be influenced by wetlands is through drinking water, with some limited exposure in bathing waters. However, drinking water is treated to a very high level, with few samples failing to meet the required standards. Bathing waters are improving in quality over the past decade and less than 5% of samples fail to meet the standards set out in legislation (DEFRA 2009). Although wetlands have the potential to improve water quality, given the high standards that can be achieved in water treatment, do wetlands have a role to play in reducing the exposure of people to pollutants and pathogens? Is the importance of wetlands confined to their role in protecting surface water quality for ecosystems rather than for people?

Certainly, wetlands can be used to reduce the overall cost of treatment, by improving the quality of pre-treatment abstracted water. The cost of removing nitrates and pesticides from drinking water has been estimated to be £7 per customer per year (Keirle and Hayes 2007). Groundwater quality problems cost the UK water industry £754 million between 1975 and 2004 (United Kingdom Water Industry Research 2004). As a result of water quality problems, 146 groundwater sources have been closed in England and Wales since 1975, which account for about seven per cent of current abstraction levels (Environment Agency 2006). The main reasons for closing these sources were due to *Cryprtosporidium* and pesticide contamination. However, even relatively contaminated water can be treated to potable standards, albeit at a high cost.

In relation to human health then, one of the main roles of wetlands is in reducing risk. Although water treatment processes are very effective, if there are failures in the system the quality of the abstracted water will determine the maximum potential exposure of people to pollutants and pathogens. Water samples for testing are typically taken at different points in the water treatment process. However, the results for microbiological test results are likely to take one day to be returned, while other more complicated tests (e.g. for pesticides) may take 10 days (Keirle and Hayes 2007), within which time the water will have entered the distribution system. There may also be other important contaminants or pathogens that are not regularly sampled for (see, for example, Chapter 6), but which the systematic action of wetlands can buffer or filter. There is a need, therefore, to address the quality of water sources in order to reduce risks to people. This general approach is formalised within Drinking Water Safety Plans (Drinking Water Inspectorate 2005). Taking a wider ecosystem approach that maintains the quality of water in the environment through retaining functioning wetland ecosystems rather than relying on water treatment in the distribution system has benefits therefore, not just for ecosystems, but also for reducing human health risks and creating robust water supply systems that are resilient to shocks and failures.

9

The Way Forward

ROGER CROFTS, THE SIBTHORP TRUST

9.1 Introduction

There is a great deal of knowledge about the link between ecosystem health and human health, but this is not used effectively in practice to improve the quality of the natural environment and to improve the life chances of citizens. Connecting the knowledge base to the practitioners and to the target human population is therefore critical. This is a key message emerging from the seminar and the selected papers presented here. Some clear connections are identified from the research reported. There is the connection between the quality of ecosystems, and particularly the goods and services that they provide, and the transmission of disease vectors from animals to humans. There is evidence that new connections between the developing world and the industrialised world are creating new problems. For example, the number of zoonoses that can be transmitted to humans is increasing through the destruction of habitats and increases in the unregulated trade of wild animals for food and as pets for citizens of industrialised countries. And rising levels of ecotourism to developing countries by citizens from industrialised countries is increasing the vulnerability of those visitors to new diseases. On the other hand, there is increasing evidence from work, in both the laboratory and in the field in the UK, that interaction with nature and activities in green space all have beneficial effects on the health of individuals: emotional, psychological, spiritual, and physical, and also on the health and functionality of human communities. Access to nature, increased access to the outdoors and especially to high quality green space, active participation in exercise in the outdoors, and the transformation of derelict and abandoned land to more aesthetically pleasing and more publicly accessible and beneficial uses, are the key components. Increasing access and engaging in these activities, in turn, reduces the likely demand on the health services and can have a major effect on the costs of the provision of health services. The papers presented here provide some of the detailed evidence base for these simple but telling overview points. The question that arises is why is this knowledge not resulting in improvements in physical and mental health of citizens?

The answer to this question appears to lie in addressing the following issues:

1. making the case for connecting people and their environment to improve human health;
2. defining the outstanding issues;
3. translating knowledge into practice; and
4. engaging the key stakeholders to bring about changes in practice.

The remainder of this chapter examines these four issues in the light of the papers presented and the discussions between participants at the seminar.

9.2 Making the case

Generally speaking, there is a clear evidence base for linking healthy human lives with healthy natural environments. There is what could be called 'a virtuous circle'. Healthy ecosystems can provide support for and improvement of human health and, in turn, an individual's engagement with the environment means that they have a greater positive feel for the environment and what should be done to improve it. There are some clear messages from available research, particularly a link between improving people's moods and self-esteem and their engagement with the natural world, and directly or indirectly with green space. It is also clear that different health conditions respond to different environmental and green space exposures and activities. Some good practice examples are provided in the foregoing chapters, especially in relation to exercise in the outdoors, development of green exercise, use of 'green gyms' and initiatives under the Co-operation on Health and Biodiversity (COHAB) programme. Two examples will suffice in this summary to underline the significance of understanding disease vectors linkages between the natural environment and humans.

The Severe Acute Respiratory Syndrome (SARS) appears to be linked to the destruction of natural habitats and consequential loss of species, and a greater degree of contact between native species and humans from industrialised countries. Also, the increasing levels of trade in bush meat and wild animals for pets, especially from south east Asia and Africa, that are both illegal and unregulated, results not only in degradation of biodiversity, but also in the introduction of disease vectors in the receiving countries.

The evidence base is gradually increasing, but the evidence available is not foolproof. There is some concern about the rigour of the research to the extent that the results could be open to question. In some cases, the research findings were not easy to defend in the face of challenge from those less than convinced about the general case of the links between healthy ecosystems and healthy human lives.

An informative example was provided from research in Sheffield that revealed the effects of shrinking recreational space. A young boy of the current generation has a very small recreation space, a few hundred metres, compared with his parents, his grandparents and his great grandparents all of whom had huge amounts of space; in each successive generation this space had diminished. It is difficult to demonstrate that this has a detrimental effect on the lifespan of the current generation, given all of the improvements in health and diet, but it was argued that lack of access to recreational space might bring about a culture that places a lower value on natural ecosystems.

A broader message on the need to reconnect society to the natural world in the UK emerged during the seminar. Individuals' perception of the natural world might not be influenced by the great natural wonders of Africa for example, but rather urban parks and other more informal open spaces, and river valleys. There is a critical message to articulate to medical and health professionals and to teachers that there are substantial social, economic and health benefits from engaging with the outdoors. Participants recognised that there are some risks, but the overwhelming evidence is that using the green option as a health cure, rather than the modern technical medical option, could save a very considerable amount of money and staff resources in the health services.

Despite one participant stating that there is sufficient knowledge of the benefits and all that is needed is more action, it is clear that the argumentation on the benefits to human well-being from access to green space needs to be developed. Participants considered that there was a need to articulate the high degree of certainty in the links between health and environment from the particular perspective of green spaces. In this context, the question arises how can environmental events affecting people be used to rekindle the link between people and the natural world. At the time of the seminar, extensive flooding in the Don valley in Sheffield was quoted as a good example of the effect on the physical and mental health, emotional well-being of individuals and how measures to stem the effect of these occurrences could have a beneficial effect on human health.

Seminar participants came from a broad spectrum of the medical and environmental fields. There was a great deal of consensus between them on the importance of linking humans with the natural world and green space to improve their life chances. This is a simple but vitally important conclusion. If individuals from the two professional perspectives are in profound disagreement, it will be very difficult to argue the case to those who are not convinced of the benefits of citizens having a more active interest in and engagement with nature and green space.

9.3 Defining the outstanding issues

The second major issue, and related to the need to make the case for the link between healthy environments and healthy human lives, is to ensure that knowledge is enhanced and the link between policy and action improved.

Many gaps in the knowledge base were identified. There is a need for hard data on how ecosystems can reduce exposure to pollutants and disease, and the role that they can have in risk mitigation. The evidence base appears to be much greater on zoonoses, and relatively poorer on pollutants. For example, a greater proportion of emerging infectious diseases discovered in recent decades are zoonoses, i.e. carry disease from nature to humans, than in the past. There are some contentious issues. Most people think, for example, that contaminated land is a health hazard, but there is apparently no proof that this is the case. Other parts of the natural environment, such as abnormally high levels of radon gas, are considered to have a greater detrimental effect on human health. The question remains should greater use be made of the 'precautionary approach' by developing its role in environment and human health.

There are many programmes to restore wetlands due to the benefits for biodiversity and to increase the ecological functioning of river systems to capture and store pollutants. However, there is little evidence available on the link between wetland restoration and human health. This is a topic requiring further investigation, and it should be linked to the role that wetlands have in river systems in the context of the EU Water Framework Directive, which ignores the function of wetlands, and the role of wetland restoration.

Another aspect requiring more detailed investigation is the potential link between disease vectors and their transmission to humans directly from animals and indirectly through the water cycle and through food chains. The lack of clarity in any causal link between MAP and Crohn's disease was quoted as an example of the need for hard data to prove whether a connection did or did not exist.

The existence of nature and the ability of humans to see it and experience it at first hand is a critical element in the healthy environment/healthy people debate. The experience of seeing animals and plants in the wild and in specially designated places, such as nature reserves, is one element. But, perhaps more important for the majority of people is the experience of green spaces and other types of open spaces in and around settlements. There are also less tangible elements of the environment, such as the goods and services it provides (for example clean water, and healthy disease-free food) which have an impact directly on human well-being and indirectly on human self esteem. For all of these elements, it is necessary to quantify the values and benefits of human interaction with green spaces using the many environmental economic evaluation methods available.

More investigation on the economic benefits of access to green spaces and to nature is needed. Particular issues identified included examining the cause/effect relationship between human well-being and access to green space, development of a greater linkage between the urban population, which is in need of access to green space, and rural areas which are the major supplier of green space. A major focus of attention should be to compare the costs of providing access to green space and nature compared to the high cost of traditional medical treatment.

The development of indicators of human health is an important component for tracking improvements. Specific action is needed to develop indicators of wellness in relation to access to green space and to interaction with the natural world. A number of proposals for indicators were discussed during the seminar and these should be taken forward. Most of the indicators are relatively easy to measure, as information already exists, but it has not been brought together in a form that enables evaluations to be undertaken.

Future research needs to be more rigorous. It is also essential that the qualitative aspects of the healthy ecosystem/healthy people linkage is investigated by social scientists. Research should also allow greater transfer from the theory to practical application. And, more interdisciplinary research would be beneficial given the complexity of the issues being dealt with and the need for bringing different perspectives to bear on practical solutions. Specific mention was made of bringing experts together representing virology, wildlife biology, disease ecology, medical practice and health care, economics and recreational provision.

An issue of continuing concern is that lack of knowledge leads to poor decisions being made. There is a requirement therefore for new knowledge to be better integrated into decision making and that all of the information available is provided to those involved in the policy-making and decision-making processes.

9.4 Translating knowledge into practice

Major improvements in human health could be achieved if the existing knowledge is applied in practice. This involves ensuring that the findings from research are used by those treating patients and by those responsible for planning and designing outdoor space.

In urban areas, urban design and urban planning could be substantially improved. The present approaches of site cramming and reclamation of all brownfield sites for building were criticised. A more balanced approach is required which recognises the importance of creating new open space and providing access to it, especially for communities that are currently deprived. One aspect that requires more consideration is the use of Strategic Environmental Assessment in all policies, programmes and plans for urban design and development to ensure that increases in the provision of green space and access to it are factored into all plans and executed in practice.

The reclamation of derelict land is an important consideration in both reducing the flow of pollutants in contact with humans and providing opportunities for the creation of green space on land that was previously regarded as waste by society. It is essential, however, that the knowledge on the best forms of remediation is applied in practice, such as appropriate vegetation cover (grass or trees dependent on the types of pollutants at the site). If this knowledge is applied, the reclamation will result in a more aesthetically pleasing area for citizens, and provide opportunities for open-air recreation, as well as creating economic development opportunities.

Beyond the urban environment, more attention is needed on providing access for urban people to the countryside and specifically giving access to nature. Those sections of the population most likely to benefit from providing this access are those who are suffering or who are vulnerable to suffering from mental health problems - young people, low income groups, ethnic minorities and those with physical disabilities.

If the disease vectors from developing countries, and especially from tropical ecosystems, are to be reduced, much greater surveillance of trade and a higher degree of regulation are required. In the UK, there remains the problem of animal-to-animal transmission of disease between different parts of the country, and therefore the possibility of infection of humans. To reduce these possibilities requires much stricter regulation of live meat and animal carcass transfers and the development of local meat processing facilities. This will have a direct cost as smaller scale processing facilities have high unit operating costs, but the biosecurity benefits for both animal and human populations will be greater than the costs of operating small scale meat processing facilities.

A basic issue that needs to be resolved is to ensure that the key experts engage with each other so that the existing knowledge is applied in practice. The most important component is considered to be improved links between recreation providers and the medical practitioners.

9.5 Influencing stakeholders

There are many constituencies of interest who should be the targets for the healthy environment/healthy people approach. In the medical field, new medical students, epidemiologists, hospital based medical staff, health care workers, public health associations, and those designing medical facilities are all important. In the environmental field, specialists in recreation and access to the countryside, in urban design and landscape architecture, and those responsible for managing and maintaining parks and gardens and other forms of public open space are targets. Beyond these specific constituencies, the business community as employers are also important. Overall, health sector businesses and health professionals are key targets on grounds that they determine the treatments and medicines.

To win the argument and improve the health of humans requires the knowledge and messages about access to green space and the reduction in zoonoses to be transmitted effectively to key stakeholders, and to be understood and acted upon by them.

One of the key targets is those that harbour the threats, and particularly those who trade in exotic animals. Both government regulatory bodies and those that understand the causes and effects, especially the scientists, have key roles to play. Raising the level of understanding of the value of ecosystems is crucial, as is the need to improve communication within multidisciplinary teams and between them and the wider world, as opposed to scientists from one laboratory just speaking to those in another about their own research. This requires better communication from scientists to the general public and involves clearly and objectively setting out the actual risks. And, it means trying to ensure that the media do not hi-jack the agenda and scare the public. There is also a need to improve the schools science curriculum, and to have up-to-date web sites, and good fact sheets available for the general public.

9.6 Overview

Where do we go from here? Is the available evidence driven by science or is it ecosystem driven? The answer is not yet clear at this stage. There is a still a major challenge of proving the link between human health, and especially reducing illness and increasing wellness, and the effective functioning of ecosystems and the health of the natural environment. How do we use the available material to get the message over in order to convert the cynics and the sceptics? There is also the important issue about societal values and beliefs: are greater links between individuals and their natural and modified environment good for them and should they be encouraged? In a sense, the debate about modern hi-tech medicine and natural remedies is a case in point. If an individual feels better having taken the latter route, is that not sufficient to encourage its use even if it only as a placebo effect? Taking the ethical approach a step further raises the interesting question of whether we should as a society take the eco-centric approach or stick to the anthropo-centric approach? There is no clear consensus on this point, but is it a choice between one or the other, or is a mixture of the two likely to be preferable? How are the barriers between different perspectives and policies broken down? Some encouragement can be taken from the existence of strategies developed at different levels of government from the national through to the local. And there is encouragement from the many examples of good practice, and many people taking action. But, it is essential to ensure that lessons are learned from all of the evidence and good practice. In particular, good practice ideas from one part of the country should be put into practice elsewhere. In this connection, bringing people together, getting them to look at initiatives that they may be then able to transfer to their own part of the world and to their own communities is extremely important. Too often, there are institutional mindsets and cultures that get in the way of making linkages across knowledge divides and across people/environmental divides. A simple phrase with deep meaning in this respect is the need to change the health agenda "from an approach focussing on illness and its cure, to one based on wellness and its encouragement". The goal should be fewer people getting ill and in need of medical treatment. Strategies which seek to cross the divide in thinking and culture do help, but only if they are understood and acted upon by all of those to which they are aimed, are backed up with targets that are measurable and supported by monitoring systems that allow progress to be measured and results broadcast.

There is a need to put together a coherent case for action using all of the research and the practical knowledge and ideas gained to date. To wait for the perfect answer from new research means that individuals who are in need of an improved life chance now will not get one. The basic requirement is for a double paradigm shift. First, is the need for a cultural change in the treatment of humans by the medical profession from an illness reduction, reactive approach to a proactive, wellness stimulation approach. Second, is the practical change from focus on high cost/high technology, and facility-based solutions to curing illness to greater dependence on low cost tailored access to green space and to nature in and around where people live and work.

10

References

Abubakar, I., Myhill, D.J., Hart, A.R., Lake, I.R., Harvey, I., Rhodes, J.M., Robinson, R., Lobo, A.J., Probert, C.S.J. and Hunter, P.R. (2007) A case-control study of drinking water and dairy products in Crohn's disease–Further investigation of the possible role of mycobacterium avium paratuberculosis. American Journal of Epidemiology, 165, 776-783.

Abubakar, I., Myhill, D., Aliyu, S.H. and Hunter, P.R. (2008) Detection of *Mycobacterium avium* subspecies *paratuberculosis* from patients with Crohn's disease using nucleic acid-based techniques: A systematic review and meta-analysis. Inflammatory Bowel Diseases, 14, 401-410.

Air Quality Expert Group (AQEG) (2005) Particulate Matter in the UK. DEFRA, London. ISBN 0-85521-143-1

Ashley, A., Bartlett, H., Lamb, S., *et al.* (2000) Evaluation of the Thames Valley Health Walks Scheme. Participant's feedback survey. OCHRAD report 9. Oxford: Oxford Centre for Health Care Research and Development.

Ayele, W.Y., Svastova, P., Roubal, P., Bartos, M. and Pavlik, I. (2005) *Mycobacterium avium* subspecies *paratuberculosis* cultured from locally and commercially pasteurized cow's milk in the Czech Republic. Applied and Environmental Microbiology, 71, 1210-1214.

Baldari, M., Tamburro, A., Sabatinelli, G., Romi, R., Severini, C., Cuccagna, G., Fiorilli, G., Allegri, M.P., Buriani, C. and Toti, M. (1998) Malaria in Maremma, Italy. Lancet 1998, v351, n 9111, pp. 1246-1247

Baldia, M. (2003) The Origins of Agriculture (v2.01), www.comp-archaeology.org/AgricultureOrigins.htm, accessed 17 Sept 2007

Barton, H. and Grant, M. (2006) A health map for the local human habitat, Journal of the Royal Society for the Promotion of Health vol. 126, no. 6.

Beckett, K.P., Freer-Smith, P.H., Taylor, G. 2000. Particulate pollution capture by urban trees: effect of species and windspeed. Global Change Biology 6, 995-1003.

Bell, D.J., Roberton, S. and Hunter, P. (2004) Animals origins of SARS coronavirus: possible links with the international wildlife trade in small carnivores. Philosophical Transactions of the Royal Society. B. 359: 1107-1114

Bell, D.J., Roberton, S. and Hunter, P. (2005) Animal origins of SARS coronavirus: possible links with the wildlife trade in small carnivores. In: SARS: A case study in emerging infections. Eds. A McLean, R May, J Pattison and R Weiss. OUP, Oxford.

Bell, D.J., Wilkinson, D. and Cunningham, A. (2005) Wild goose chase? The Parliamentary Monitor, 133, 56-57

Berger, M., Speare, R., Daszak, P., Green, E. and Cunningham, A. (1998) Chrytridiomycosis causes amphibian mortality associated with population declines in the rain forests of Australia and Central America. Proceedings of the National Academy of Sciences USA 95: 9031-9036

Bird, W. (2007) Natural Thinking. A Report by Dr William Bird, for the Royal Society for the Protection of Birds, Investigating the links between the Natural Environment, Biodiversity and Mental Health. RSPB

Blancou, J., Chomel, B.B., Belotto, A. and Meslin, F.X. (2005) Emerging or re-emerging bacterial zoonoses: factors of emergence, surveillance and control. Veterinary Research 36: 507-522

Boldeman, C., Dal, H., and Wester, U., (2004) Swedish pre-school children's UVR exposure – a comparison between two outdoor environments. Photodermatol Photoimmunol Photomed 20 (1) p 2 - 8.

Broadmeadow, M., Beckett, P., Jackson, S., Freer-Smith, P. and Taylor, G. (1998) Trees and pollution abatement. In: Forest Research Annual Report and Account 1997-1998. The Stationery Office, Edinburgh.

Bunbury, N., Barton, E., Jones, C., Greenwood, A., Tyler, K. and Bell, D.J. (2007a) Avian blood parasites in an endangered columbid: *Leucocytozoon marchouxi* in the Mauritian Pink Pigeon Columba *mayeri*. Parasitology 134 (6): 797-804

Bunbury, N., Jones, C.G., Greenwood, A.G. and Bell, D.J. (2007b) *Trichomonas gallinae* in Mauritian columbids: implications for an endangered endemic. *Journal of Wildlife Diseases* 43: 399-407

Bunbury, N., Jones, C.G., Greenwood, A. and Bell, D.J. (2008a) Epidemiology and conservation implications of *Trichomonas gallinae* in the endangered Mauritian pink pigeon. *Biological Conservation* 141: 153-161.

Bunbury, N., Jones, C.G., Greenwood, A. and Bell, D.J. (2008b) Causes of mortality in free-living Pink pigeons *Columba mayeri* 2002-2006. Endangered Species Research

Centers for Disease Control and Prevention (CDC) (2003) Reptile-associated salmonellosis-selected stats 1998-2002. MMWR Morb Mortal Wkly Rep. 52:1206-1209

Charrel, R.N. and Lamballerie, X. (2003) Arenaviruses other than Lassa virus. Antiviral Research 57:89-100

Chin, T. and Welsby, P.D. (2004) Malaria in the UK: past, present, and future. Postgraduate Medical Journal 2004; 80:663-666

Chiodini, R. J., Vankruiningen, H. J. and Merkal, R. S. (1984) Ruminant Para-Tuberculosis (Johnes Disease) – The Current Status And Future-Prospects. Cornell Veterinarian, 74, 218-262.

Chomel, B.B., Belotto, A. and Meslin, F.X. (2007) Wildlife, exotic pets and emerging zoonoses. Emerging Infectious Diseases 13: 6-11

Chorus, I. and Bartram, J. (eds.) (1999) Toxic cyanobacteria in water: A guide to their public health consequences, monitoring and management. WHO ISBN 0-419-23930-8

Cimprich, B. (1993) Development of an intervention to restore attention in cancer patients, Cancer Nursing 16 (1993), pp. 83-92.

Cirone, K., Morsella, C., Romano, M. and Paolicchi, F. (2007) *Mycobacterium avium* subsp. *paratuberculosis* in food and its relationship with Crohn's disease. Reviews of Argentinian Microbiology, 39, 57-68.

Coley, R.L., Kuo, F.E., and Sullivan, W.C. (1997) Where does community grow? The social context created by nature in urban public housing. Environment and Behavior, 29(4), 468-494.

Cooper, M. E. and Rosser, A.M. (2002) International regulation of wildlife trade: relevant legislation and organisations. Revue Scientifique Et Technique De L Office International Des Epizooties, 21 (1). pp. 103-123. ISSN 0253-1933

Costanza, R., Farber, S.C. and Maxwell, J. (1989) Valuation and Management of Wetland Ecosystems. Ecological Economics. 1: 335-361.

Dahlgren, G. and Whitehead, M. (1991) Policies and strategies to promote social equity in health, Institute of Future Studies, Stockholm

Daszak, P., Cunningham, A.A. and Hyatt, A. (2000) Emerging infectious diseases of wildlife-threats to biodiversity and human health. Science 287:443-449

Daszak, P., Tabor, G.M., Kilpatrick, A.M., Epstein, J. and Plowright, R. (2004) Conservation medicine and a new agenda for emerging diseases. Annals of the New York Academy of Science 1026:1-11

De Munck, C.S., Hutchings, T.R. and Moffat, A.J. (2008). Impacts of climate change and establishing a vegetation cover on water erosion of contaminated spoils for two contrasting UK regional climates – a case study approach. Integrated Environmental Assessment and Management. 2008 Oct;4(4):443-55.

de Vries, S., Verheij, R.A., Groenewegen, P., and Spreeuwenberg, P. (2003) Natural environments – healthy environments? An exploratory analysis of the relationship between greenspace and health. Environment and Planning 35 p1717 - 1731.

Department for Environment, Food and Rural Affairs (DEFRA) National Emergency Epidemiology Group (2005) Epidemiology Report on Avian Influenza in a Quarantine Premises in Essex, DEFRA, London.

Department for Environment, Food and Rural Affairs (DEFRA) (2007). A Strategy for England's Trees, Woods and Forests. DEFRA, London.

Department for Environment, Food and Rural Affairs (DEFRA) (2009) www.defra.gov.uk accessed 23/1/09

10. References

Department of Health (DoH) (2004a) At least five a week: Evidence on the impact of physical activity and its relationship to health. Department of Health; Physical Activity; Health Improvement and Prevention: Chief Medical Officer, Department of Health: 1–128.

Department of Health (DoH) (2004b) Choosing Health? Choosing Activity: a consultation on how to increase physical activity, HMSO London.

Department of the Environment, Transport and the Regions (DETR) (2000) DETR Circular 2/2000 Contaminated Land: Implementation of Part IIA of the Environmental Protection Act 1990. The Stationery Office, London.

Diette, G.B., Lechtzin, N., Haponik, E., Devrotes, A. and Rubin, H.R. (2003) Distraction therapy with nature sights and sounds reduces pain during flexible bronchoscopy: a Complimentary Approach to Routine Analgesia. Chest 2003; 123;941–948.

Dobson, A. and Foufopulous, J. (2001). Emerging infectious pathogens of wildlife. Philisophical Transactions of the Royal Society B. 356:1001–1012

Duckworth, J.W., Salter, R.E. and Khounboline, K. (compilers) (1999) Wildlife in Lao PDR: 1999 Status Report. Vientiane: IUCN–The World Conservation Union / Wildlife Conservation Society / Centre for Protected Areas and Watershed Management.

Drinking Water Inspectorate (DWI) (2005) A Brief Guide to Drinking Water Safety Plans.

Drinking Water Inspectorate (DWI) (2007) Drinking water 2006. Drinking water in England and Wales ISBN 978–1–905852–11–6

Environment Agency (2006) Underground, under threat: The State of Groundwater in England and Wales. Environment Agency. 2006

Ellingson, J.L.E., Anderson, J.L., Koziczkowski, J.J., Radcliff, R.P., Sloan, S.J., Allen, S.E. and Sullivan, N.M. (2005) Detection of viable *Mycobacterium avium* subsp *paratuberculosis* in retail pasteurized whole milk by two culture methods and PCR. Journal of Food Protection, 68, 966–972.

English Partnerships (2007a) National Brownfield Strategy – Recommendations to Government. English Partnerships, London.

English Partnerships (2007b) National Land Use Database of Previously Developed Land (NLUD–PDL). Summary of 2006 Data Returns – Distribution of Previously Developed Land. English Partnerships, London.

Eves, H.E. and Ruggiero, R.G. (2000) Socioeconomics and the sustainability of hunting in the forests of northern Congo (Brazzaville). pp. 427–454 In: Robinson, J.G. and Bennett, E.L. (eds.) Hunting for sustainability in tropical forests. Columbia University Press, New York

Fa, J., Peres, C. and Meeuwig, J. (2002). Bushmeat exploitation in tropical forests: an intercontinental comparison. Conservation Biology 16:232–237

Fa, J.E., Ryan, S.F. and Bell, D.J. (2005) Hunting vulnerability, ecological characteristics and harvest rates of bushmeat species in afrotropical forests. Biological Conservation 121: 167–176

Farago, M., Thornton, I., Kavanagh, P., Elliott, P., Leonardi G.S. (1997) Health aspects of human exposure to high arsenic concentrations in soil in south–west England. In: Arsenic: Exposure and health effects. Abernathy, C.O., Calderon, R.L. and Chappell, W.R. (eds.). Kluwer Academic Publishers.

Fevre, E. *et al.* (2006) Animal movements and the spread of infectious diseases. Trends in Microbiology 14: 125–131

Field, K.G. and Samadpour, M. (2007) Fecal source tracking, the indicator paradigm, and managing water quality. Water Research, 41, 3517–3538.

Fisher, J. and Acreman, M.C. (2004) Wetland nutrient removal: a review of the evidence. Hydrology and Earth System Sciences, 8(4), 673–685.

Foley, S.L., Lynne, A.M. and Nayak, R. (2009) Molecular typing methodologies for microbial source tracking and epidemiological investigations of Gram–negative bacterial foodborne pathogens. Infection, Genetics and Evolution, Volume 9, Issue 4, July 2009.

Foster, G.R. (2004) User's Reference Guide for RUSLE2 (Draft). USDA-Agricultural Research Service, Washington, DC, USA.

Freer-Smith, P.H., Holloway, S., Goodman, A. (1997) The uptake of particulates by an urban woodland: site description and particulate composition. Environmental Pollution 95, 27-35.

Freer-Smith, P.H., El-Khatib, A.A. and Taylor, G. (2004). Capture of particulate pollution by trees: A comparison of species typical of semi-arid areas (*Ficus nitida* and *Eucalyptus globulus*) with European and North American species. Water Air and Soil Pollution 155, 173-187.

Friend, M. (1995) Increased avian diseases with habitat change. pp. 401-403 In: LaRoe, E., Farris, G., Puckett, C., Doran P. and Mac M. (eds.) Our Living Resources: a report to the nation on the distribution, abundance and health of US plants, animals and ecosystems. US Department of the Interior, National Biological Service, Washington, D.C.

Fuller, R.A., Irvine, K.N., Devine-Wright, P., Warren, P.H., and Gaston, K.J. (2007) 'Psychological benefits of greenspace increase with biodiversity', Biological Letters, August 22; 3(4): 390-394

Gadepalle, V.P., Ouki, S.K., van Herwijnen, R., Hutchings, T.R. (2006) Novel technique for sustainable brownfield remediation of arsenic contaminated soils, Oral presentation at the 22nd annual international conference on soils, sediments and water, Amherst, Massachusetts.

Garcia-Aymerich, J., Farrero, E., Felez, M.A., *et al.* (2003) Risk Factors of readmission to hospital for COPD exacerbation: A prospective study. Thorax 2003;58:100-5

Gaspar da Silva, D., Barton, E., Bunbury, N., Lunness, P., Bell, D.J. and Tyler, K.M. (2007) Molecular identity and heterogeneity of Trichmonad parasites in a closed avian population. Infection, Genetics and Evolution 7: 433-440

Giles-Corti, B., Timperio, A., Bull, F., and ; Pikora, T. (2005) Understanding Physical Activity Environmental Correlates: Increased Specificity for Ecological Models. Exercise and Sport Sciences Reviews. 33(4):175-181, October 2005.

Gill, J., Webby, R., Gilchrist, M. and Gray, G. (2006) Avian influenza among waterfowl hunters and wildlife professionals. Emerging Infectious Diseases 12: 1284-1286

Gilliver, M., Bennett, M., Begon, M., Feore, S.M. and Hart, C.A. (1999) Antibiotic resistance found in wild rodents. Nature 401 233-234.

Greene, S., Yartel, A., Moriarty, K., Nathan, L., Salehi, E. *et al.* (2007) *Salmonella* Kingabwa infections and lizard contacts, United States, 2005. Emerging Infectious Diseases 13: 661-662

Hahn, B., Shaw, G., De Cock, K.M. and Sharp, P. (2000) AIDS as a zoonosis: scientific and public health implications. Science 28 January 2000: Vol. 287. no. 5453, pp. 607 - 614

Halliwell, E. (2005) Up and Running? Exercise therapy and the treatment of mild or moderate depression in primary care. London, Mental Health Foundation.

Harrison, C., Burgess, J., Millward, A. and Dawe, G. (1995) Accessible Natural Greenspace Standards in Towns and Cities: A Review of Appropriate Size and Distance Criteria. English Nature Research Report 153. Peterborough.

Hartig, T., Evans, G., Jamner, L.D., Daviss, D.S., and Garling, T. (2003) Tracking restoration in natural and urban field settings, Journal of Environmental Psychology, vol 23, pp109-123

Herzog, T.R., Black, A.M., Fountaine, K.A. and Knotts, D.J. (1997) Reflection and Attention Recovery as distinctive benefits of restorative environments. J Environmental Psychology 17 165-170.

Hildebrand, H., Finkel, Y., Grahnquist, L., Lindholm, J., Ekbom, A. and Askling, J. (2003) Changing pattern of paediatric inflammatory bowel disease in northern Stockholm 1990-2001. Gut, 52, 1432-1434.

Huynh, N.V. and Hai, T.T (2002) Survey and observation on the nuisance mosquitoes for inhabitants of Tram Chim and Lang Sen Reserves of the Plain of Reeds. In: Decision-support system for implementing ecosystem-based wetland management through functional zonation of land use. Project Final Report. Department for International Development Project R7544.

10. References

James, C., Fisher, J., Russell, V., Collings, S. and Moss, B. (2005) Nitrate availability and hydrophyte species richness in shallow lakes. Freshwater Biology 50, 1049–1063.

Jensenius, M., Fournier, P., Kelly, P., Myrvang, B. and Raoult, D. (2003). African tick bite fever. Lancet Infectious Diseases 3: 557–64

Jerozolimskia, A. and Peres, C. (2003) Bringing home the biggest bacon: a cross-site analysis of the structure of hunter-kill profiles in neotropical forests. Biological Conservation 111: 415–425

Jezek, Z., Arita, I., Mutombo, M., Dunn, C., Nakano, J. and Szczeniowski, M. (1986) Four generations of probable person-to-person transmission of human monkeypox. American Journal of Epidemiology. 123:104–1012

Jones, K.E., Patel, N.K., Levy, M.A., Storeygard, A., Balk, D., Gittleman, J.L. and Daszak, P. (2008) Global trends in emerging infectious diseases Nature 451: 990–994

Jones, J.G., Simon, B. and Orlandi, M.J.L.G. (1979) A Microbiological Study of Sediments from the Cumbrian Lakes. J Gen Microbiol, 115, 37–48.

Kaplan, R. and Kaplan, S. (1995) The experience of nature: A psychological perspective. New York: Cambridge University Press.

Kaplan, S. (1995) The restorative benefits of nature: toward an integrative framework, Journal of Environmental Psychology, vol 15, pp169–182

Karesh, W.B, Cook, R.A., Bennett, E.L., Newcomb, J. (2005) Wildlife trade and global disease emergence. Emerging Infectious Diseases 11: 1000–1002.

Kerile, R. and Hayes, C. (2007) A review of catchment management in the new context of drinking water safety plans. Water and the Environment Journal 21 (2007) 208–216.

Knox, A.K., Dahlgren, R.A., Tate, K.W. and Atwill, E.R. (2008) Efficacy of Natural Wetlands to Retain Nutrient, Sediment and Microbial Pollutants. Journal of Environmental Quality 2008 37: 1837–1846.

Kovats, S. and Jendritzky, G. (2006) Heatwaves and human health. In Menne, B. and Ebi, K.L. (eds) Climate Change and adaptation strategies for human health. World Health Organisation, Geneva, Switzerland.

Land Use Consultants (2008) Understanding the relevance and application of the Access to Natural Green Space Standard. Report prepared for Natural England by Land Use Consultants.

Lau, S.K., Woo, P.C., Li, K.S., Huang, Y., Tsoi, H.W., Wong, B.H., Wong, S.S., Leung, S.Y., Chan, K.H. and Yuen, K.Y. (2005). Severe acute respiratory syndrome coronavirus-like virus in Chinese horseshoe bats. Proceedings of the National Academy of Sciences, U.S.A. 102: 14040–14045.

Leroy, E., Rouquet, P., Formenty, P., Souquiere, S., Kilbourne, A., Froment et al. (2004) Multiple Ebola virus transmission events and rapid decline of central African wildlife. Science 303: 387–390

Li, W. et al. (2005) Bats are natural reservoirs of SARS-like coronaviruses Science 310: 676–679

Lindgren, E. and Jaenson, T.G.T. (2006) Lyme borreliosis in Europe: influences of climate change, epidemiology, ecology and adaptation measures. In Menne, B. and Ebi, K.L. (eds) Climate Change and adaptation strategies for human health. World Health Organisation, Geneva, Switzerland.

Maller, C., Townsend, M., Brown, P. and St Leger, L. (2002) Healthy Parks, Healthy People: the health benefits of contact with nature in a park context: an annotated bibliography. Deakin University and Parks, Victoria, Australia.

Masuzawa, T. et al. (2006) Leptospirosis in squirrels imported from United States to Japan. Emerging Infectious Diseases 12: 1153–1155.

Mayberry, J.F. (1989) Recent epidemiology of ulcerative colitis and Crohn's disease in Cardiff. Internatiuonal Journal of Colorectal Disease, 4, 39–46.

Mayberry, J.F. and Hitchens, R.A.N. (1978) Distribution of Crohn's disease in Cardiff. Society, Science and Medicine, 12, 137–138.

Mayberry, J., Rhodes, J. and Hughes, L.E. (1979) Incidence Of Crohn Disease In Cardiff Between 1934 And 1977. Gut, 20, 602-608.

McCrone, P., Dhanasiri, S., Patel, A., Knapp, M. and Lawton-Smith, S. (2007) Paying the price. The cost of mental health care in England to 2026. King's Fund.

Meays, C.L., Broersma, K., Nordin, R. and Mazumder, A. (2004) Source tracking fecal bacteria in water: a critical review of current methods. Journal of Environmental Management, 73, 71-79.

Midgley, J., Ashton, N., Casstles, H., McNamara, J., Tocque, K., Bellis, M. (2005) Health, Environment and Deprivation in the North West of England. Centre for Public Health, Liverpool John Moores University, UK.

Millar, D., Ford, J., Sanderson, J., Withey, S., Tizard, M., Doran, T. and Hermontaylor, J. (1996) IS900 PCR to detect Mycobacterium paratuberculosis in retail supplies of whole pasteurized cows' milk in England and Wales. Applied and Environmental Microbiology, 62, 3446-3452.

Millennium Ecosystem Assessment (MEA) (2005). Ecosystems and Human Well-Being: Synthesis. Island Press, Washington. 155pp.

Milner-Gulland, E.J. and Bennett, E.L. (2002) Annual meeting Wild Meat, Wild meat: the bigger picture, Trends in Ecology and Evolution, 2003, Vol: 18, Pages: 351 – 357, ISSN: 0169-5347

Mind (2007) Ecotherapy: The green agenda for mental health. Mind week report, May 2007. www.mind.org.uk/mindweek

Mitchell, R. and Popham, F. (2008) Effect of exposure to natural environment on health inequalities: an observational population study, The Lancet, vol 372, pp1655-60

Mortimore, J.L. (2007) Environmental Impact assessment of Water, Sediment and Airborne Particles in the Tamar River Catchment. PhD Thesis, University of Reading, UK.

Mura, M., Bull, T.J., Evans, H., Sidi-Boumedine, K., McMinn, L., Rhodes, G., Pickup, R. and Hermon-Taylor, J. (2006) Replication and long-term persistence of bovine and human strains of Mycobacterium avium subsp paratuberculosis within Acanthamoeba polyphaga. Applied and Environmental Microbiology, 72, 854-859.

Murphy F. (1998). Emerging zoonoses. Emerging Infectious Diseases. 4:429-435

Nakamura, R. and Fujii, E. (1990) Studies of the Characteristics of the Electroencephalogram When Observing Potted Plants: Pelargonium Hortorum 'Sprinter Red' and Begonia Evansiana. Technical Bulletin of the Faculty of Horticulture of Chiba University, Vol. 43, pp. 177-183. (In Japanese with English Summary).

Naser, S.A., Schwartz, D. and Shafran, I. (2000) Isolation of Mycobacterium avium subsp paratuberculosis from breast milk of Crohn's disease patients. American Journal of Gastroenterology, 95, 1094-1095.

ODPM (2003) Sustainable communities: building for the future. Office of the Deputy Prime Minister, London.

Office for National Statistics (2000) UK Time Use Survey.

Oostvogel, P.M., van Doornum, G., Ferreira, R., Vink, J., Fenollar, F. and Raoult, D. (2007) African tickbite fever in travellers, Swaziland. Emerging Infectioius Diseases 13: 353-355

O'Reilly, C.E., O'Connor, L., Anderson, W., Harvey, P., Grant, I.R., Donaghy, J., Rowe, M. and O'Mahony, P. (2004) Surveillance of bulk raw and commercially pasteurized cows' milk from approved Irish liquid-milk pasteurization plants to determine the incidence of Mycobacterium paratuberculosis. Applied and Environmental Microbiology, 70, 5138-5144.

Ostrowski, S., Leslie, M., Parrott, T., Abelt, S. and Piercy P. (1998) B-virus from pet macaque monkeys: an emerging threat in the United States? Emerging Infectious Diseases 4:117-121

Peres, C. (2000) Effects of subsistence hunting on vertebrate community structure in Amazonian forests. Conservation Biology 14: 240-253

10. References

Pettit, C., Azapagic, A., Robins, A., Sinnett, D., Poole, D., Chalabi, Z., Fletcher, T., Jones, M. and Cleall, P. (2006) Integrated Assessment of Pollutants in the Urban Environment. Collaborations Across the Divide, RGS–IBG Annual Conference 2006, Kensington Gore, London, 30th August – 1st September 2006

Pickup, R.W. (1995) Sampling and detecting bacterial populations in natural environments. In: Baumberg, S., Young. J.P.W., Wellington. E.M.H. and Saunders, J.R. (eds.) Population Genetics of Bacteria. Cambridge University Press, Cambridge. ISBN 0 521 48052 3

Pickup, R.W., Rhodes, G. and Hermon–Taylor, J. (2003) Monitoring bacterial pathogens in the environment: advantages of a multilayered approach. Current Opinion in Biotechnology, 14, 319–325.

Pickup, R.W., Rhodes, G., Arnott, S., Sidi–Boumedine, K., Bull, T.J., Weightman, A., Hurley, M. and Hermon–Taylor, J. (2005) *Mycobacterium avium* subsp *paratuberculosis* in the catchment area and water of the river Taff in South Wales, United Kingdom, an its potential relationship to clustering of Crohn's disease cases in the city of Cardiff. Applied and Environmental Microbiology, 71, 2130–2139.

Pickup, R.W., Rhodes, G., Bull, T.J., Arnott, S., Sidi–Boumedine, K., Hurley, M. and Hermon–Taylor, J. (2006) *Mycobacterium avium* subsp *paratuberculosis* in lake catchments, in river water abstracted for domestic use, and in effluent from domestic sewage treatment works: Diverse opportunities for environmental cycling and human exposure. Applied and Environmental Microbiology, 72, 4067–4077.

Pongsiri, M.J. and Roman, J. (2007) Examining the Links between Biodiversity and Human Health: An Interdisciplinary Research Initiative at the U.S. Environmental Protection Agency. Ecohealth 4(1): pp82–85.

Pretty, J., Griffin, M., Peacock, J., Hine, R., Sellens, M. and South, N. (2005a) A countryside for Health and Well-Being: The Physical and Mental Health Benefits of Green Exercise. Report for Countryside Recreation Network. Feb 2005.

Pretty, J., Hine, R. and Peacock, J. (2006) Green Exercise: The benefits of activities in green places. The Biologist 53(3), 143–148

Pretty, J., Peacock, J., Hine, R., Sellens, M., South, N. and Griffin, M. (2007) Green exercise in the UK Countryside: effects on health and psychological well–being, and implications for policy and planning. Journal of Environmental Planning and Management 50 (2) 211–231

Pretty, J., Peacock, J., Sellens, M. and Griffin, M. (2005b) The mental and physical health outcomes of green exercise. International Journal of Environmental Health Research 15(5), 319–337.

Pretty, J. (2007) The Earth Only Endures: On Reconnecting with Nature and our Place in it. Earthscan, London.

Prior, H. and Johnes, P.J. (2002) Regulation of surface water quality in a Cretaceous Chalk catchment, UK: an assessment of the relative importance of instream and wetland processes. The Science of the Total Environment 282–283 (2002) 159–174

Promed (2007) Chikungunya – Italy (Emilia Romagna) (04) 20070907.2957 www.promedmail.org

Reed, K.D., Melski, J., Graham, M., Regnery, R., Sotir, M., Wegner, M. *et al.* (2004) The detection of monkeypox in humans in the Western Hemisphere

Renou, C., Cadranel, J–F, Bourliere, M., Halfon, P. *et al.* (2007) Possible zoonotic transmission of Hepatitis E from pet pig to its owner. Emerging Infectious Diseases 13: 1094–1096

Reynolds, M., Davidson, W., Curns, A., Conover, C., Huhn, G., Davis J. *et al.* (2007) Spectrum of infection and risk factors for human monkeypox, United States, 2003. Emerging Infectious Diseases 13: 1332–9

Riley, P.Y. and Chomel, B.B. (2005) Hedgehog zoonoses. Emerging Infectious Diseases. 2005;11:1–5.

Roberton, S.I., Bell, D.J., Smith, G.J.D., Nicholls, J.M., Chan, K.H., Dzung, N.T., Tran, P.Q., Streicher, U., Poon, L.L.M., Chen, H., Horby, P., Guardo, M., Guan, Y. and Peiris J.S.M. (2006) Avian Influenza H5N1 in Viverrids: implications for wildlife health and conservation. *Proceedings of the Royal Society Lond Series B.* 273: 1729– 1732

Robinson, J.G. and Bennett E.L. (eds.) (2000) Hunting for sustainability in tropical forests. Columbia University Press, New York

Roddy, E., Zhang, W. and Doherty, M. (2005) Aerobic walking or strengthening exercise for osteoarthritis of the knee? A systematic review. Annals of the Rheumatic Diseases 2005;64:544–548

Rouquet, P., Froment, J.M., Bermejo, M., Yaba, P., Délicat, A., Rollin, P.E. and Leroy E.M. (2005) Wild Animal Mortality Monitoring and Human Ebola Outbreaks, Gabon and Republic of Congo, 2001-2003. Emerging Infectious Diseases Vol. 11, No. 2, February 2005

Rozak, D.B. and Colwell, R.R. (1987) Survival strategies of bacteria in the natural environment. Microbiological Reviews, 51, 365–376.

Scanu, A.M., Bull, T.J., Cannas, S., Sanderson, J.D., Sechi, L.A., Dettori, G., Zanetti, S. and Hermon-Taylor, J. (2007) *Mycobacterium avium* subsp *paratuberculosis* infection in cases of irritable bowel syndrome and comparison with Crohn's disease and Johne's disease: Common neural and immune pathogenicities. Journal of Clinical Microbiology, 45, 3883-3890.

Scottish Executive (2006) The Scottish Forestry Strategy. Forestry Commission Scotland, Edinburgh.

Sempik, J., Aldridge, J., and Becker, S. (2002) Social and therapeutic horticulture: evidence and messages from research., Thrive and CCFR, Loughbrough University.

Sport England (2007) The Active People Survey Technical Report. Prepared for Sport England by Ipsos MORI.

Staats, H. and Hartig, T. (2004) Alone or with a friend: A social context for psychological restoration and environmental preferences. Journal of Environmental Psychology, Volume 24, Issue 2, June 2004, pp 199-211

Swift, L., Hunter, P.H., Lees, A. and Bell, D.J. (2007) The wildlife trade and the emergence of infectious diseases Ecohealth 4: 25-30

Takahashi, K., Kitajama, N., Abe, N. and Mishiro, S. (2004) Complete or near-complete nucleotide sequences of hepatitis E virus genome recovered from a wild boar, a deer and four patients who ate the deer. Virology 330: 501-505

Takano, T., Nakamura, K. and Watanabe, M. (2002) Urban residential environments and senior citizens' longevity in megacity areas: the importance of walkable green spaces. Journal of Epidemiology and Community Health (56): 913 -918.

Taylor, L., Latham, S. and Woolhouse, M. (2001) Risk factors for human disease emergence. Phil.Trans. R. Soc. Lond. B. 356:983-989

The National Assembly for Wales (2001) Woodlands for Wales. Forestry Commission Wales, Aberystwyth.

The Sainsbury Centre for Mental Health (2003) The economic and social costs of mental illness. London.

Turner, R.K., Dent, D. and Hey, R.D. (1983) Valuation of the environmental impact of wetland flood protection and drainage schemes. Environment and Planning A 15(7) 871 – 888

Ulrich, R.S. (1981) Natural versus urban scenes: some psychological effects. Environment and Behaviour 13 p523 -556

Ulrich, R.S. (1984) Post operative results following Gallbladder surgery in 23 matched pairs of patients. View through a window may influence recovery from surgery. Science 224,420-421.

Ulrich, R.S., Simons, R.F., Losito, B.D., Fiorito, E., Miles, M.A. and Zelson. M. (1991) Stress Recovery during exposure to natural and urbal environments. Journal of Environmental Psychology, Vol 11, pp.201-230.

United Kingdom Water Industry Research (2004) Implications of changing groundwater quality for water resources and the UK water industry, Phase III: Financial and water resources impact. UKWIR, London, 70pp.

10. References

Van Borm, S., Thomas, I., Hanquet, G., Lambrecht, B., Boschmans, M., Dupont, G., Decaestecker, M., Snacken, R. and van den Berg, T. (2005) Highly pathogenic H5N1 virus in smuggled Thai eagles Belgium. Emerging Infectious Diseases 11: 702–706

van den Berg, A.E., Hartig, T. and Staats, H. (2007) Preference for nature in urbanized societies: stress, restoration, and the pursuit of sustainability. Journal of Social Issues, vol 63, no 1, pp79–96

van Herwijnen, R. *et al.* (2007a) The effect of organic materials on the mobility and toxicity in contaminated soils. Applied Geochemistry. Volume 22, Issue 11, November 2007, Pages 2422–2434

van Herwijnen, R. *et al.* (2007b) Remediation of metal contaminated soil with mineral-amended composts. Environmental Pollution. Volume 150, Issue 3, December 2007, Pages 347–354

Verhoeven, J.A.T. and Mueleman, A.F.M. (1999) Wetlands for wastewater treatment: Opportunities and limitations. Ecological Engineering 12 5–12

Vijaykrishna, D., Smith, G.J., Zhang, J.X., Peiris, J.S., Chen, H. and Guan, Y. (2007) Evolutionary insights into the ecology of coronaviruses. Journal of Virology. 81:531–545

Vorou, R.M., Papavassiliou, V.G. and Tsiodras, S. (2007) Emerging zoonoses and vector-borne infections affecting humans in Europe. Epidemiology and Infection, Volume 135, Issue 08, Nov 2007, pp 1231–1247.

Wanless, D. (2002) Securing our future health: Taking a Long-Term View. HM Treasury.

Wells, N.M. and Lekies, K.S. (2006) Nature and the life course: Pathways from childhood nature experiences to adult environmentalism. Children, youth and environments 16(1).

Wilson, E.O. (1984) Biophilia, Harvard University Press, Cambridge

Wolfe, N., Switzer, W., Carr, J., Bhullar, V., Shanmugam, V., Tamoufe, U. *et al.* (2004) Naturally acquired simian retrovirus infections in central African hunters. 363:932–937

Wolfe, N., Daszak, P., Kilpatrick, A. and Burke, D. (2005) Bushmeat hunting, deforestation and prediction of zoonotic disease. Emerging Infectious Diseases. 11: 1822–1827

World Health Organization (2005) Ecosystems and human well-being: health synthesis: a report of the Millennium Ecosystem Assessment, World Health Organization, Geneva, Switzerland

Xu, Y., Lou, Z., Liu, Y. Pang, H., Tien, P., Gao, G. and Rao, Z. (2004) Crystal structure of Severe Acute Respiratory Syndrome Coronavirus Spike protein fusion core. The Journal of Biological Chemistry 279 (47): 49414–49419.